Animal Rights: A Very Short Introduction

'. . . introductions to this increasingly important topic don't come much better than this book by David DeGrazia . . . thorough, compelling and well written, explaining the capabilities of animals, and emphasizing the gap between how we ought to treat animals and the often appalling reality of how we do treat them.'
Robert Garner, University of Leicester

'Historically aware, philosophically sensitive, and with many well-chosen examples, this book would be hard to beat as a philosophical introduction to animal rights.'
Roger Crisp, Oxford University

Very Short Introductions available now:

For more information visit our web site:
www.oup.co.uk/general/vsi/

David DeGrazia

ANIMAL RIGHTS

A Very Short Introduction

OXFORD
UNIVERSITY PRESS

OXFORD
UNIVERSITY PRESS

Great Clarendon Street, Oxford OX2 6DP

Oxford University Press is a department of the University of Oxford.
It furthers the University's objective of excellence in research, scholarship,
and education by publishing worldwide in

Oxford New York

Auckland Bangkok Buenos Aires Cape Town Chennai
Dar es Salaam Delhi Hong Kong Istanbul Karachi Kolkata
Kuala Lumpur Madrid Melbourne Mexico City Mumbai Nairobi
São Paulo Shanghai Taipei Tokyo Toronto

Oxford is a registered trade mark of Oxford University Press
in the UK and in certain other countries

Published in the United States
by Oxford University Press Inc., New York

British Library Cataloguing in Publication Data
Data available

Library of Congress Cataloging in Publication Data
Data available
ISBN 987-0-19-285360-8

10

Typeset by RefineCatch Ltd, Bungay, Suffolk
Printed in Great Britain by
Ashford Colour Press Ltd, Gosport, Hampshire

For Kathleen, my soulmate and partner-in-life,
and for our precious little Zoë

Contents

List of illustrations

Preface
and acknowledgements

In writing this book on animal rights, I have naturally given voice to my own understanding of the associated issues. For this reason, I cannot claim to address these issues with perfect neutrality. I argue not only that sentient animals have moral status, but also that they are due equal consideration (in a specific sense of this term that is explained in Chapter 2). At the same time, because I find another view – the 'sliding-scale model' – to be almost as compelling, throughout the book I track the implications of both of these views about animals' moral status. But, finding the view that sentient animals entirely lack moral status to be virtually indefensible, after attempting to refute this view I largely leave it behind.

Some years before taking up the present project I completed the much longer and more scholarly *Taking Animals Seriously: Mental Life and Moral Status* (Cambridge: Cambridge University Press, 1996). Whereas that book was mainly addressed to an academic audience, the present book is written for all thoughtful people who wish to learn about ethical and philosophical issues connected with animal rights. Accordingly, I have written *Animal Rights: A Very Short Introduction* as accessibly as I could manage without oversimplification; I have also introduced each chapter with one or more vignettes and have included, for each chapter, a list of references, sources, and (in some cases) recommended further readings, rather than formal footnotes. For those who have read *Taking*

Animals Seriously, it may be of interest that the present book includes an historical overview of attitudes about animals, a discussion of the different senses of 'animal rights', and a detailed examination of the animal research issue – extending the discussion beyond the terrain covered in the earlier work.

As I complete this book, I would like to express my gratitude to several individuals who have helped along the way. At Oxford University Press, George Miller, Editorial Director for Trade Books, invited me to submit a proposal and helped with the initial brainstorming; later, Rebecca O'Connor and Catherine Humphries provided much assistance with editorial details. Robert Garner served as an external reviewer of a draft of the manuscript, offering much encouragement and several helpful criticisms and suggestions. I have also benefited from discussions with Bernard Rollin about animals' mental lives, with Paul Shapiro about activism on behalf of animals, and with Peter Singer about a variety of ethical issues involving animals. Finally, I would like to thank my entire family, and especially Kathleen and Zoë, for their love and support.

David DeGrazia   Washington, DC, July 2001

Chapter 1
Introduction

Acting on an anonymous tip in April 2001, Compassion Over Killing (COK), a Washington, DC-based animal rights organization, began investigating an enormous industrial hen house owned by agricultural company ISE-America in Cecilton, Maryland. After ISE officials ignored their request for a tour, COK activists surreptitiously entered the facility at night with video cameras. The video footage, which COK representatives later revealed at a press conference, shocked many viewers. Those present saw thousands of hens, many featherless and apparently dying, crowded into small 'battery' cages made of wire and stacked atop one another. Some birds were covered in faeces; several were immobilized, caught in cage wires. A few of the chickens appeared to be dead and decomposing. The activists, who freed eight chickens – judged to be in very poor health by a local veterinarian – are, at the time of this writing, mobilizing a national campaign to ban battery cages. Thus, their target is not ISE in particular, whose facility is fairly typical, but rather the egg production system as a whole.

Such campaigns by animal activists have sometimes been successful. Facing pressure from activists, the European Union has decided to phase out battery cages by 2012. And, in summer 2000, McDonald's announced that its restaurants would purchase eggs only from suppliers who give hens 72 square inches of cage space – almost 50 per cent more than the American industry standard.

1. An animal rights activist videotaping the inside of a factory farm.

These events reflect a major cultural phenomenon: the emergence of the contemporary animal rights movement, which has challenged long-standing, traditional views about non-human animals' moral status. Most people are opposed to cruelty and sense that animals have moral significance. At the same time, traditional views that sanction animal use with few constraints have deeply influenced our beliefs and everyday practices. The moral and intellectual tension one can experience in the face of such conflicting beliefs motivates an effort to sort out these issues. How should we understand the moral status of animals *vis-à-vis* human beings? Traditionalists and champions of animal rights generally agree that the answer has much to do with how we should understand animals themselves: What kinds of beings are animals and, in particular, what are their mental lives like?

In addressing these and related issues, it will be helpful to begin with a historical sketch both of traditional thinking about animals and of the emergence of the animal rights movement. The following sketch (which is influenced by Bekoff, Egonsson, Regan and Singer, and especially Taylor – see 'References, sources, and further reading') is quite compressed and therefore necessarily selective in identifying principal sources of traditional and current attitudes about animals.

Historical sketch

Throughout the world, chief sources of traditional thinking about animals' moral status have been religion and philosophy, both of which have interacted with science in shaping conceptions of what sorts of beings animals are. It is worth noting, however, that the tendency to distinguish philosophy and religion is primarily Western, while the distinction between philosophy and science is relatively modern. In the West, Aristotle influentially argued that animals, having sense perception but lacking *reason*, fall below humans in a natural hierarchy and are therefore appropriate resources for human purposes. Because animals lack rational souls, he contended, our dealings with them are not a matter of justice. Aristotle also held that men are naturally superior to women, due to men's allegedly superior reasoning ability, and that some humans – stronger in body than in mind – are naturally suited to be slaves. Among the ancient Greeks, dissenting voices included those of Pythagoras, who believed that animals may be former humans reincarnated, and Theophrastus, who thought animals were capable of some degree of reasoning. But most subsequent Western philosophers and theologians have concurred with Aristotle's thesis that animals exist for the use of humans, who alone are rational.

The Bible largely reinforced the Aristotelian view of animals by asserting that God created humans in his own image, and that we are free to use natural resources – including animals – for our own purposes. On the other hand, by declaring that *all* humans are made in God's image, the Bible legitimated an egalitarian view of humanity that opposed the

3

aristocratic tendencies of Greek thought, including Aristotle's. In the Middle Ages, such Christian philosophers as Augustine and Thomas Aquinas underscored the claim that animals' lack of reason justified their subordination – a thesis most Christians have accepted ever since. While agreeing that animals are subordinate to humans, the more ancient tradition of Judaism has placed greater importance than has Christianity on minimizing pain caused to animals. Based on the idea that all God's creatures deserve compassion, this concern finds expression in Jewish prescriptions regarding the slaughter of animals for food and in condemnation of hunting for pleasure, bullfights, and dogfights. Meanwhile, Islam, the third Abrahamic religious tradition, concurs that humans are uniquely important and that animals exist for human use. Still, the Koran forbids cruelty to animals and arguably suggests (depending on one's reading) that animals possess some degree of rationality; moreover, the Prophet Muhammad allegedly commented, 'Whoever is kind to the creatures of Allah, is kind to himself.'

While revealing interesting differences among its representatives, Western modern philosophy – the era stemming from Descartes in the seventeenth century through the late nineteenth century – largely upheld the view of human supremacy, reflecting the influence of its dominant religion, Christianity. Conceptualizing nature in purely mechanical terms, modern science replaced the long-dominant Aristotelian view of nature as endowed with purposes and somewhat akin to a living being. With this background, Rene Descartes found it natural to regard animals, part of nature, as organic machines, entirely devoid not only of reason but of *feelings*. Humans bodies, he thought, were part of nature, whereas the essence of humanity – revealed through a unique capacity for language and innovative behaviour – was found in the human mind, spirit, or soul, which alone possessed consciousness. That animals could not even feel pain, however, struck most philosophers as contrary to common sense. Hence Thomas Hobbes, John Locke, Immanuel Kant, and others attributed perception and feelings to animals while denying that they had some property – such as reason or the capacity to grasp general concepts – that was allegedly necessary for significant moral status. In Kant's enormously influential moral philosophy, *autonomy*, or freedom from the causal determinism of nature, became prominent in justifying the human use of animals.

While the assertion of human superiority clearly dominated modern philosophy, the possibility of alternative perspectives was also evident. A partial example is found in David Hume, who, regarding sympathy as a fountain of moral thought, noted that sympathy can extend to sensitive creatures other than humans. Still, Hume thought, the notion of justice concerns transactions among those roughly equal in power and is therefore irrelevant in our dealings with animals. More radical was the pioneering utilitarian Jeremy Bentham, who held that right conduct was a matter of maximizing the balance of pleasure over pain in those affected by one's action. Quietly noting an implication of this standard in a footnote, Bentham asserted that the principle of utility must take into account sentient animals, who can experience pleasure and pain, no less than human beings; thus he castigated the routine infliction of suffering on animals as human 'tyranny'. The later utilitarian John Stuart Mill proffered a more complex notion of utility, in which human-typical pleasures – such as intellectual, aesthetic, and moral enjoyments – carried greater weight in the calculation of utility than did common sensuous pleasures. This theoretical move back in the direction of human superiority, however, did not blind Mill to the tension between everyday animal-using practices and an impartial moral standpoint that takes animals' interests into account. The comparatively unorthodox Arthur Schopenhauer, meanwhile, rejected reason, autonomy, self-consciousness, and power as primary determinants of moral status. Influenced by Hinduism and Buddhism, Schopenhauer maintained that moral living requires compassion for all beings who can suffer. Nevertheless, in his view, human beings' greater intelligence increases their capacity for suffering and to that extent justifies heightened moral concern for human suffering.

In the arena of modern science, the greatest contribution to our understanding of animals was the nineteenth-century work of Charles Darwin, who demonstrated that humans evolved from other animal species. He also argued powerfully, if less influentially, that animals' and humans' capacities differ largely in degree and not in kind. Based on careful observations, Darwin contended that many animals possess general concepts, some reasoning ability, rudiments of moral sentiments, and complex emotions. While scientists have largely ignored these Darwinian claims until quite recently, the theory of evolution – especially in combination with modern genetics – has made the assertion of some unbridgeable cognitive gulf dividing humans and other animals much more difficult to sustain.

Our historical sketch has thus far examined only the Western tradition. Before turning to the animal rights movement(s) of the nineteenth and twentieth centuries, let us consider some leading ideas from non-Western traditions, which in some cases provide interesting contrasts with Western thought.

While a Westerner and an Easterner may both speak of life as sacred, only the Easterner is likely to have in mind *all* life. The Indian traditions of Jainism, Hinduism, and Buddhism all accept, in some form, the doctrine of *ahimsa*, which advocates non-injury to all living things and reverence for all life; these traditions also share a belief in reincarnation. Jains and Buddhists emphasize the interconnectedness of living things, recommend vegetarianism, and oppose traditional practices of animal sacrifice. Hinduism, which really comprises several distinct religions, has changed considerably in recent centuries due partly to the influence of Buddhists and Jains. *Ahimsa* has become more central in Hinduism while animal sacrifice has become less common. Many Hindus today believe that harming life will result in later suffering for the agent, grounding a strong animal-protection ethic in self-interest. Meanwhile, in the Far East, the ancient but still living tradition of Confucianism stresses a unity of all things in nature and perceives only differences in degree between human and animal capacities. Accordingly, followers of Confucius, despite granting humans significant priority, cultivate feelings of oneness with all life and sympathy for all beings who suffer.

On the American continents, the native peoples (who probably originated from Asia, crossing from present-day Russia to Alaska) tend to see nature as animated by spirit – in dramatic contrast to Descartes's mechanistic conception of nature. In keeping with their spiritual view of animal life, Native Americans generally accept some principle of respect for animals, while permitting the (respectful) killing and consumption of them.

In sum, the Western tradition has largely upheld the view that human beings have exclusive, or at least radically superior, moral status on the premiss that only humans are autonomous, rational, self-aware, or capable of understanding justice. Animals are generally seen as existing for human use. Non-Western traditions display significant differences both among themselves and in contrast to the West. Viewing them collectively, one often finds two strands pulling in different directions: a serious commitment to protecting animal welfare and respecting animal life – whether that life is valued intrinsically or as a means to one's own salvation and flourishing – but also the conviction that humans are more important than other animals.

While the Western tradition has generally been less respectful than non-Western traditions towards animals, it has been in the West that the contemporary idea and politics of animal rights have emerged. The first significant animal rights movement began in nineteenth-century England, where the impetus was opposition to the use of unanaesthetized animals in scientific research. This movement inspired protests, legislative reforms in the United Kingdom, and the birth of numerous animal-protection organizations, primarily in the English-speaking world. But opposition to animal research declined early in the twentieth century and, despite the continuation of some of the early humane organizations, the movement lost momentum and became less visible to the public eye.

In the 1960s and 1970s, the political and intellectual climate in Great Britain, the United States, and several other Western countries was receptive to a new humane movement. The civil rights movement's opposition to racial and sexual discrimination opened a door to rejecting other forms of discrimination. Concerns about pollution and destruction of the environment created logical and cultural room for heightened concern for individual animals, who are obviously affected by the state of the environment. In science, the once-dominant theory of behaviourism – which prohibits discussion of 'inner states' of animals (and humans), making it difficult for compassion towards animals to find a scientific foothold – was beginning its protracted demise. In 1976, Donald Griffin published *The Question of Animal Awareness*, marking the birth of an increasingly influential scientific movement: cognitive ethology, which studies animal behaviour in the context of evolutionary theory and posits such 'inner states' as beliefs, desires, and feelings. And the publication in 1975 of Peter Singer's *Animal Liberation*, which combined powerful philosophical reasoning with accessible writing, was a key event. This book inaugurated an explosion of rigorous philosophical literature on the moral status of animals – a topic that twentieth-century philosophers generally neglected – while inspiring many people to become activists on behalf of animals.

It was within this receptive cultural space that the recent animal rights movement emerged. Important developments included the formation of the British Hunt Saboteurs Association in 1963 and the founding of the environmental group Greenpeace in 1971 and of People for the Ethical Treatment of Animals in 1980. Today the animal rights movement includes hundreds of organizations, millions of members, and some considerable legislative breakthroughs – such as the highly progressive Swedish Animal Welfare Act (1988), the British Veal Crate Ban (1990), and the International Dolphin Conservation Act (1992), to name just a few. In the scientific community, the study of alternatives to animal research has become respectable in some quarters. And whereas individuals who abstained from meat on ethical grounds appeared eccentric twenty or thirty years ago, moral vegetarianism has entered the mainstream and is spreading rapidly.

Thus Western culture has changed, becoming more receptive to the idea of animal rights and more serious in exploring associated issues regarding animals' moral status and mental lives. We are no longer surprised to see animal activists on the news. Many people today are grappling with questions concerning the proper treatment of animals. They want to improve their understanding and appreciation of the issues associated with animal rights.

Plan for the book

Several key issues will be identified in this book. The most fundamental questions concern animals' moral status *vis-à-vis* human beings. Do animals have any moral status or moral rights? What do these terms mean, exactly? If animals have moral status or rights, should we regard them as equal, in some morally relevant sense, to human beings? Here it will be necessary to distinguish equal treatment from equal consideration, and to outline different views on these issues. Also, we must confront an issue of scope. Which animals do we have in mind in talking about 'animals' – literally all animals, including amoebas, just sentient animals (who have feelings), or some other group? We confront these issues in Chapter 2.

Discussions of animals' moral status often make the common-sense assumption that many animals are sentient. But any detailed, careful examination of ethical issues involving animals requires knowing more about what animals – especially their minds – are like. For example, if one thinks that shrimp lack sentience, having no (conscious) sensations at all, that belief may undercut moral concern for these creatures. The basic question of Chapter 3, therefore, is this: based on available empirical evidence, roughly what set of animals appear to have *feelings* – sensations such as pain, and emotional states such as fear – and what sorts of feelings do they have?

With a clearer understanding of animals' mental lives, we address in Chapter 4 the question of what sorts of *interests* animals have. Put another way, we seek an account of the major ways in which animals can be *harmed*. Plainly, unpleasant feelings such as pain and distress are a type of harm. Animals can also be harmed by *confinement* – restrictions of liberty that significantly interfere with an individual's ability to live well. But is the interest in avoiding confinement just an instance of the interest in avoiding unpleasant feelings? Or do we harm a caged animal who doesn't suffer from captivity, being accustomed to it, by eliminating opportunities for species-typical functioning? And does premature *death*, as distinguished from an unpleasant dying process, harm an animal? Does killing a normal, healthy dog painlessly in her sleep harm the dog? Once we begin to probe the nature of animals' interests, and the general ways in which animals can be harmed, we encounter matters of genuine controversy. The discussion of this chapter will indicate different ways of viewing these issues, suggesting answers to some of them.

Chapters 2 to 4 set up the more practical discussions in the chapters that follow, by providing frameworks for understanding animals' moral status, mental lives, and interests. Chapter 5 examines the ethics of meat-eating. It focuses on the issue of consuming meat produced in factory farms, but also takes up the issues of eating meat produced in family farms and eating seafood. In Chapter 6, we investigate the ethics of keeping pets and zoo animals. In addition to considering the harms often imposed upon these animals, the chapter addresses whether there are legitimate objections – based on *respect* for animals – against restricting their liberty at home or in zoos. Finally, Chapter 7 explores the exceptionally complex issue of animal research. It confronts such topics as these: whether biomedical progress justifies harming non-consenting research subjects; if so, whether there is a degree of harm to animal subjects beyond which it is unethical to go; how promising a proposed experiment must be to be ethically defensible; and how aggressively the research community should pursue alternatives to animal use.

If this book is successful, it will help the reader navigate through several leading issues at the centre of contemporary discussions of animal rights.

Chapter 2
The moral status of animals

Each Labor Day from 1934 to 1998, a live animal shooting festival took place in the small town of Hegins, Pennsylvania (USA), before the event was banned. Participants travelled from around the globe to take part. In the annual event, some 5,000 pigeons were released from traps, one by one, only to become targets for participants. Most of the birds who were shot – more than three-quarters, according to investigators for The Fund for Animals – were wounded but not immediately killed. Some would be left on the shooting fields as each contestant completed his or her round of shooting, while some would escape to nearby woods to die slowly from their wounds. After each round was completed, young children collected injured birds and killed them by stomping on them, ripping off their heads, smashing them against the sides of barrels, or tossing them into barrels to suffocate among other dying or dead pigeons. The shooters and children did not carry out these activities in secrecy. Thousands of spectators paid admission to sit in bleachers, eat, drink beer, and roar their approval for the shooters and children.

One may occasionally hear the claim that human use of animals raises no ethical issues whatsoever. If that is correct, then none of the actions just described – shooting live pigeons for fun, stomping them to death, tearing off their heads, and so on – is morally problematic. Nor, for that matter, is encouraging children to take part in cruelty to animals, or encouraging both adults and children to engage in such cruelty by paying for admission.

It is difficult to imagine a less plausible moral position. It is difficult to imagine any morally serious person – any person, that is, who thinks it important to act rightly and not wrongly – who would not condemn at least some of the actions just described for causing extensive, unnecessary harm to the birds. While the attitude of completely dismissing animals as morally insignificant may have been more common in centuries past (see Chapter 1), this attitude is becoming increasingly rare, suggesting a form of moral progress. Still, as the pigeon shoot illustrates, plenty of people remain willing to inflict cruelty on animals.

Clearly, at least some of the ways the pigeons were treated in the annual hunt were wrong. If one argues that *shooting* birds for fun is not so obviously wrong, because with luck the target will be instantly killed (ignoring the fact that many of those shot were not so lucky), such a defence will offer no comfort to those hoping to justify, say, tossing injured birds into barrels to suffocate among other birds. Such treatment of birds – and other sentient animals – is wrong. But *why* is it wrong? And what does the answer suggest about the *moral status* of animals and whether they have *rights*? The remainder of this chapter will discuss various possible answers to these questions.

Moral status

Increasingly many people claim that animals have moral status, moral rights, or both. Before determining whether such claims are correct, we need to know what they mean. Let us begin with moral status.

To claim that a dog, for example, has *moral status* is to say that the dog has moral importance in her own right and not simply in relation to humans. More precisely, it is to say that the dog's interests or welfare

13

matters and must be taken seriously – independently of how the dog's welfare affects human interests. To put it simply, we should treat the dog well *for the dog's sake*. Consider some examples.

Reasonable people know that brutally kicking dogs for fun is wrong. Why is it wrong? Suppose Ben and Greg have different reasons for agreeing with this judgement. Ben thinks dog-kicking is wrong because it damages some pet-owner's property – suggesting *the pet-owner's interests* are the relevant factor. Of course, many dogs are no one's property. Ben might reply that kicking dogs for fun is wrong, in any case, because it is cruel – and that cruelty is a vice we should not cultivate, through cruel acts, *because having this vice makes one more likely, in the long run, to mistreat humans.* In short, abusing animals makes one the sort of person who is more likely to abuse humans. Here again human interests are Ben's ultimate basis for opposing cruelty to animals. On this view, animals' interests have no *independent* moral significance, meaning animals have no moral status.

Judging that animals do have moral status, Greg takes a different view. He believes it is wrong to kick dogs for fun because doing so harms them for no good reason. (In a different scenario, a good reason might be the fact that harming a dog is the only way to prevent her from savaging a child.) From Greg's standpoint, the dog's welfare counts in its own right; it has moral importance, independently of how human interests might be furthered by promoting the dog's welfare. Thus, even if you could convince him that abusing the dog would have no negative impact on humans, Greg would still consider the action wrong. The dog, he thinks, has moral status. (Whether the dog has *the same* moral status as all other morally significant beings, including humans, is a distinct issue.)

What, then, about *moral rights*? What does it mean to say that animals have such rights? This conceptual issue is complex because the term 'moral rights' is used in different ways. But it helps to be clear about what it means in a given context, so that people who discuss whether animals (or humans) have moral rights do not talk at cross purposes by using the term in different ways.

We can usefully distinguish three senses of 'right(s)'. (Let us assume throughout our discussion that, unless otherwise indicated, we are considering *moral*, as opposed to *legal*, rights.) In a rather loose sense of the term, to say a being has rights is simply to say the being has moral status. Call this *the moral-status sense* of 'rights'. In this sense, one could believe that dogs have moral status – but less moral status than humans – and still allow that dogs have rights; any degree of moral status would suffice. One might assert, for example, that dogs have rights not to be caused to suffer and not to be killed, meaning that these interests are morally important in their own right and should not be overridden *without good reason* – while interpreting 'good reason' broadly enough to include a company's financial interest in testing new cosmetics for toxicity. So, to say animals have rights in the moral-status sense is hardly radical.

In a second, stricter sense of 'rights' – call it *the equal-consideration sense* – to say someone has rights is to say that she deserves equal consideration. This means that her interests count as much as anyone's comparable interests. Thus, to say that dogs deserve equal consideration to humans is to assert that, for example, a dog's interest in avoiding suffering is as morally important as a human's interest in avoiding suffering; animal suffering counts as much as human suffering. If Greg judges that dogs have moral status but do not deserve equal consideration, Greg would believe that dogs have rights in the moral-status sense but not in the more radical equal-consideration sense. (Equal consideration will be further clarified later in this chapter.)

In a third, still stricter sense of 'rights' – call it *the utility-trumping sense* – to say that someone has a right to something means that, at least generally, the vital interest in question must be protected even when

15

protecting it might be disadvantageous to society as a whole. (Tom Regan and Evelyn Pluhar defend animal rights in this sense; we may call views like theirs *strong animal-rights views*.) For example, the idea that people have a moral and legal right to a fair trial means that it would be wrong to frame an innocent person, even if authorities have no true suspect and there would be great social utility in satisfying the community's desire for a conviction. While a champion of rights in this strong sense may allow that there are *some* cases in which people may override someone's rights for the common good, she would insist that such cases are exceptional and that generally appeal to the common good is insufficient to override rights.

By contrast, consider Sue, who as a *utilitarian* believes that the right action is that which is likely to maximize utility – that is, the balance of benefits over harms – considering together the interests of everyone affected, including animals. Sue believes that, while animals and humans deserve equal consideration – everyone's comparable interests count equally – we may override someone's interests when doing so is likely to maximize utility. So she holds that animals and humans have rights in the equal-consideration sense but not in the utility-trumping sense. Rights in the utility-trumping sense would provide absolute, or nearly absolute, protections of individuals' vital interests. Whether even humans have rights in this sense, however, is somewhat controversial; utilitarians, such as Peter Singer and Ray Frey, deny that they do.

We have now clarified three senses of the term 'rights'. Do animals actually have rights in any of these senses? Consider first the loose, moral-status sense. Surely, at least some of the ways in which pigeons were treated in the annual hunt were wrong, and kicking dogs for fun is wrong. Yet neither these judgements nor the more general judgement that gratuitously harming animals is wrong entails that animals have moral status. Why not?

According to *the indirect-duty view*, our moral obligations or duties are directed only towards other human beings; any obligations regarding animals, such as not to cause them needless suffering, are grounded entirely in human interests, such as the advantages to humans of not fostering cruelty. On this view, then, if there were no good reason to think that cruelty to animals is disadvantageous to humans, there would be no moral basis for condemning cruelty to animals. This is the position of Ben and the philosopher Immanuel Kant (see Chapter 1).

I contend that the indirect-duty view is false, as suggested by its inability to make sense of our obligations towards animals. First, what is decisive in condemning cruelty to animals, I suggest, is the fact that one is *needlessly harming animals*; that feature alone makes an action wrong. Second, while we are very sure that cruelty to animals is wrong – even Ben and Kant display no doubts on this score – we can't be so sure that cruelty to animals has pernicious consequences for humans. The assumption that it does depends on empirical evidence,

2. A polar bear catching a fish in her mouth.

but it is not as if those who judge that cruelty to animals is wrong can cite supporting evidence as compelling and certain as the moral judgement itself. And might it not go the other way around sometimes? Perhaps kicking his sheep around will allow the shepherd to blow off some steam, making him *less* likely to rough up his wife and kids. Moreover, cruelty to animals would presumably be wrong even in hypothetical situations in which harmful consequences for humans were *impossible* (say, if one were the last living person on Earth).

These reflections suggest that, contrary to the indirect-duty view, animals have moral status – and therefore rights in at least one sense of the term. But this conclusion leaves open the question of how much moral consideration, in comparison with humans, animals deserve and whether they have rights in a stronger sense.

A type of equality for animals?

Some animal advocates claim that 'all animals are equal'. Their opponents often reply that this is obvious nonsense. But whether or not it is nonsense depends in part on what sort of moral equality, and which particular animals, one has in mind.

A claim of moral equality on behalf of animals is surely not plausible if one means literally *all* animals, including centipedes, slugs, and amoebas. For it is extremely doubtful that such creatures are *sentient*. Sentience is more than the capacity to respond to stimuli; it is the capacity to have at least some *feelings*. Feelings include (conscious) sensations such as pain – where 'pain' refers to something *felt* and not merely the nervous system's detection of noxious stimuli – and emotional states such as fear. We do not know at what point on the phylogenetic scale, or evolutionary tree, sentience disappears, being replaced by more primitive, non-conscious neural mechanisms. But, as we will see in Chapter 3, there is strong evidence that at least vertebrate animals are sentient and little or no evidence that the most primitive invertebrates are sentient. The reason for emphasizing sentience is that non-sentient beings – lacking any capacity to feel, think, or have any other mental states – are incapable of ever caring about how they are treated. It is therefore doubtful that they can be harmed or benefited in any morally important way.

Thus, it is contrary to common sense to say that literally *all* animals are subject to some form of moral equality. What about the claim that all sentient animals are equal? Now we must ask, equal in what sense? Surely equal *treatment* for all sentient animals is not sensible, because animals have different characteristics that underlie different sorts of interests. While cats have an interest in humane treatment and liberty of movement, normal human beings also have an interest in learning how to read and developing their own life plans; we would not further cats' interests by treating them as potential readers or life planners. Moreover, a principle of respect for autonomy applies to human beings, when they achieve sufficient maturity, but does not apply to animals (with extremely few, if any, exceptions). That is why it is unobjectionable to take a cat in one's care to the veterinarian, even if the cat strongly resists, whereas it would be morally problematic to force a competent adult human to go to the doctor. These points undermine the idea that sentient animals should be given equal treatment.

On the other hand, the claim that sentient animals deserve equal *consideration* is within reason. This claim entails that wherever a human and an animal have a comparable interest, we should regard the animal's interest and the human's interest as equally morally important. To apply this idea, first we need to determine whether we have a case of comparable interests between humans and animals: do the human and animal have roughly the same thing at stake? Consider the interest in avoiding suffering. A defining feature of suffering is that it is highly unpleasant, aversive, or 'negative' from the standpoint of the subject who suffers. Suffering lowers one's experiential well-being or quality of life while one suffers. It seems plausible, then, that all beings capable of suffering have a comparable interest in not suffering. If sentient animals deserve equal consideration, then *a cow's interest in not suffering is as morally important as a human's interest in not suffering* – though different equal-consideration theories, such as utilitarianism and strong animal-rights views, will interpret this judgement in slightly different ways. If equal consideration should not extend to sentient animals, then a cow's suffering matters less than a human's suffering. (Unless otherwise indicated, the word 'animals' will hereafter refer to sentient animals in particular.)

Three increasingly strong senses of 'animal rights'

The moral-status sense

Animals have at least some moral status. Animals do not exist solely for human use, so they should be treated well for *their own* sake.

The equal-consideration sense

We must give equal moral weight to humans' and animals' comparable interests. For example, animal suffering matters as much as human suffering.

The utility-trumping sense

Like humans, animals have certain vital interests that we must not override (with few if any exceptions) even in an effort to maximize utility for society. For example, animals have a right to liberty, meaning we should not harmfully confine them even if doing so would predictably bring about many benefits and few costs.

If people generally accepted equal consideration for animals and acted accordingly, human–animal interactions would be very different. In animal husbandry, animal research, bullfights and rodeos, most circus acts involving animals and zoo exhibits, nearly all hunting, and many other practices and institutions of animal use, we do not grant animals' interests anything like equal consideration. So accepting this principle would be radical. Radical or not, from an ethical standpoint the question is whether equal consideration for animals is right. In my view, it is.

The issue of equal consideration

Like humans, animals have interests and can be benefited or harmed. Indeed, as already argued, animals have moral status. So the principle of equal consideration *could* be meaningfully applied not only to humans, but also to animals. But *should* it be? Well, it is only logical that this principle – giving everyone's comparable interests equal moral weight – should apply to all beings who have interests, *unless there is a relevant difference between the beings in question that justifies unequal consideration*. Thus, in considering whether equal consideration should extend to animals, it makes sense to begin with a presumption of equal consideration and then ask whether any arguments, citing relevant differences between humans and animals, should lead us to overturn that presumption.

If the appropriateness of a presumption in favour of equal consideration is not obvious, consider the alternative: beginning with a presumption that animals deserve less-than-equal consideration. On this approach, despite acknowledging that animals have moral status, we may *begin* by assuming that it is right to give their interests in liberty of movement, not suffering, etc. less importance than we give our comparable interests *without providing any justification for discounting their interests in this way*. That, I suggest, is unfair and wrongheaded.

21

Two equal-consideration theories

Utilitarianism

The right action or policy is that which maximizes the balance of benefits over harms, where the interests of all affected parties – including both humans and animals – are impartially considered.

Strong animal-rights view

Animals, like humans, have rights in the utility-trumping sense (see box entitled 'Three increasingly strong senses of "animal rights"' on p. 20)

This approach is especially suspect when we consider the history of human attitudes towards animals – which reveals a pronounced tendency to exploit animals and discount their moral status (see Chapter 1) – and the continuing likelihood of pro-human, anti-animal prejudice. People tend to think, rightly or wrongly, that their interests often conflict with those of animals – in such contexts as meat-eating, animal research, and pest control – and that therefore taking animals very seriously is disadvantageous to humans. So we must not ignore the likelihood of self-interested, pro-human bias. Moreover, animals are in many ways very different from us and are, with notable exceptions, not part of our social groups. But we know from experience that people often discriminate against individuals whom they perceive as different and not 'one of us', especially if the outsiders are easily dominated. Thus, anti-animal prejudice is probable. The history and continuing likelihood of such biases make a presumption of unequal consideration too inviting of moral error.

This combination of logical and pragmatic considerations favours a presumption of equal consideration for animals. This means that the *inegalitarian*, the person who favours unequal consideration for animals, has a burden of proof: identifying a relevant difference between humans and animals that justifies less-than-equal consideration for animals. I doubt the inegalitarian can shoulder this burden. But in the remainder of this section, we will encounter five major challenges to equal consideration as well as rebuttals to those challenges.

Appeals to species

The inegalitarian might defend unequal consideration for humans and animals by arguing as follows. Humans are different from animals simply on account of being human – that is, members of the *Homo sapiens* species. By definition, this species difference is a fact that uniquely identifies all and only humans, and it is morally important. It is not that some trait associated with normal members of the species – such as rationality or moral agency – grounds unique moral status; simply being human does. This we know because it is self-evident.

It can be difficult to argue against claims of self-evidence, because such claims tend to cut off further argument: 'That's just how it is, a basic moral fact, so I can't give you further justification.' Still, there are several ways to challenge appeals to species.

First, the claim that the moral significance of species is self-evident can be put in doubt by noting that many people, especially those who have thought long and hard about the moral status of animals, do *not* find the claim self-evident. The inegalitarian might reply with a charge of moral blindness – 'I can't help it if you can't see what's obvious' – but this begins to sound dogmatic. Generally, where reasonable people disagree that some claim is self-evident, explicit justification for the claim is in order. But there *is* no further justification on the present view.

Worse, the claim that the biological matter of species difference has such moral importance proves very implausible when we consider certain biological facts. We are very closely related to the two species of chimpanzee – common chimps and pigmy chimps (bonobos); our difference from each in terms of distinct DNA (about 1.6 per cent) is barely twice the difference between the two chimp species (0.7 per cent). Moreover, there have been hominid species other than *Homo sapiens*, such as *Homo erectus*, *Homo habilis*, and *Australopithecus robustus*; these hominids were more closely related to us than are chimpanzees and the other Great Apes, gorillas and orang utans. It is hardly plausible that membership in *Homo sapiens* could justify special moral status when various other species have been so similar to us. Indeed, there is no bright biological line between our species and whatever hominid species we evolved from; surely no magical mutation separated 'us' from 'them'. So why should only our species have special moral status?

Now the inegalitarian might shift ground, stating that the relevant sense of 'human' is *hominid* and that being a hominid confers special moral status. But this move is undercut by considering how slight the biological differences must have been between the most primitive hominids and the most closely related non-hominid primates. Moreover, it is quite possible that today's language-trained apes are more intellectually advanced than the most primitive hominids were, casting further doubt on the thesis that *all and only* hominids have special moral status. Besides, even if we insisted that biological differences themselves were morally important, why assume that the human/non-human divide is crucial? Why not consider all hominids plus the Great Apes to occupy the charmed circle? Or all primates? Or mammals? While we're at it, why not all vertebrates? Since species is not the only biologically meaningful grouping, it becomes clear that we must turn away from claims of self-evidence and towards developed arguments for and against equal consideration.

That these arguments will take us beyond appeals to species can be seen by considering the possible future scenario in which we encounter extraterrestrial beings who are more intelligent, sensitive, and cultured than we. If one claimed that the mere fact that they were not human justified discounting their interests, this would invite the charge of bigotry not unlike racism and sexism. Indeed, one of the biggest difficulties with the appeal to species is that it offers no more justification for its favoured way of dividing 'us' from 'them' than dogmatic racists and sexists offer for their different ways of dividing up the moral world. We may conclude, then, that appeals to species offer no prospect whatsoever for justifying less-than-equal consideration for animals.

Contract theory

Another possible way to defend unequal consideration appeals to a tradition in ethics known as *contract theory*. According to contract theory, one's moral rights and obligations flow from the terms of an agreement reached by imaginary contractors, who bargain with each other in an attempt to find mutually advantageous principles and rules by which to govern their society and structure its basic institutions. Because animals are not rational agents of the sort who can participate in designing a contract, the argument goes, animals lack moral status – from which it follows that they are not due equal consideration.

This effort to justify unequal consideration has two major problems. First, it cannot adequately account for our obligations toward animals. Indeed, its implication that animals have no moral status whatever reveals that the contract approach is implausible from the start; we have already found that the wrongness of cruelty to animals is adequately explained only by accepting that animals have moral status.

Noting the strong intuitive pull towards the conclusion that animals have moral status, Peter Carruthers has tried to account for our obligation not to be cruel to animals with a version of the indirect-duty view. Cruelty to animals, he argues, makes the agent a vicious person who is more likely in the long run to mistreat humans. We have already seen that arguments of this type are unpromising for at least the reason that they try to base a very certain moral judgement – that cruelty to animals is wrong – on speculative empirical assumptions about an undesirable spillover effect on humans. But we might take the critique a step further, for the indirect-duty view leaves unexplained *why* cruelty to animals is a vice and compassion to them a virtue. Animals, on this view, lack moral status and cannot be directly wronged. So why should pulverizing cows for fun reveal a defective moral character any more than does tearing up a newspaper for fun? The only plausible account of why cruelty is a vice acknowledges the moral status of its victims.

The contract approach faces another major problem: the thesis that moral status requires rational agency has unsettling implications regarding non-rational humans. For if this thesis is true, then human beings who lack the degree of rationality needed to understand the terms of a social contract would also lack moral status. Obviously, human infants lack such rationality but are thought to possess moral status. If the contract theorist replies that babies have the *potential* to develop into rational agents, the same may be said for human foetuses, so the appeal to potential implies that even early foetuses have moral status and deserve equal consideration. Some contract theorists will accept this implication, but many will not.

Rather than pursuing the issues of infants' and foetuses' moral status, let us consider those human beings who lack even the potential for moral agency (and never had it earlier) – for example, the most severely retarded humans. On the present view, they apparently lack moral status and may be treated accordingly. Carruthers has attempted to block this unpalatable implication in two ways, however.

First, he offers a *slippery slope argument* as follows. If we don't treat non-rational humans such as the severely retarded *as if they had rights* – he conflates the moral-status and equal-consideration senses of this term – we will open the door to the abuse of those humans who just barely satisfy the rationality criterion, who really do have rights. We are imprecise judges of the capabilities that make up rational agency, so in practice we almost certainly would not draw exactly the right line between those who do and those who do not satisfy the standard. To avoid sliding down the slope of such fine-grained discriminations into abuse of right-holders, we should stay out of the business of deciding which humans are rational.

This argument has several difficulties. First, while not unreasonable, the assumption that we would bungle the task of assigning rationality is speculative. Surely it is less certain than the moral judgement it is supposed to support – that it would be wrong to treat non-rational humans as if they lacked moral status (for example, coercing them into harmful experimentation, killing them for their transplantable organs). Second, consider a hypothetical scenario in which we gained the ability to make impeccable discriminations of rationality. Even if this occurred, would it not still be wrong to treat non-rational humans as lacking moral status? Such humans really do have moral status and *that* is why it is wrong to treat them as if they didn't.

Carruthers also offers an *appeal to social stability*. It is a psychological fact, he argues, that many people would be extremely distressed if we denied rights to non-rational humans and would be unable to comply with such a policy, regardless of its justification. So, in order to avoid the social instability that would otherwise result, we must *confer* rights on non-rational humans. But the problems with this argument parallel those of the previous one. First, its assumption that treating non-rational humans as lacking moral status would lead to social instability is speculative and, at best, less certain than the moral conviction that such humans shouldn't be treated this way. Second, it seems unable to handle the moral intuition that, in a hypothetical scenario in which people were not upset by treating the non-rational as lacking rights, it would nevertheless be wrong to treat them this way.

In conclusion, the contract approach wrongly denies that animals have moral status and does not adequately account for the moral status of non-rational humans. It therefore fails to overturn the presumption in favour of equal consideration for animals.

Appeals to moral agency

Rather than appealing to contract theory, which in turn invokes the concept of a rational agent, the inegalitarian might appeal directly to *rational agency* or *moral agency* (terms I will use interchangeably). The contention is that one must be a moral agent in order to have full moral status and deserve equal consideration. But how can one justify this claim? Some inegalitarians assert that it is *intuitively* justified. Others invoke a *principle of reciprocity*: one can have moral rights, or deserve equal consideration, only if one has moral obligations, and only moral agents have such obligations. If some rights-bearers had no moral obligations, they would reap the advantages of moral protection without the burden of having moral responsibilities (obligations) – and that, the argument goes, is unfair to moral agents, who carry that burden. However the inegalitarian justifies the claim that moral agency confers rights, she maintains that human beings are moral agents while animals, or at any rate the vast majority of them, are not.

This last assertion, however, immediately provokes the problem that some human beings lack even the potential for moral agency, and the present approach can handle the problem of non-paradigm humans no better than contract theory can. Additionally, like contract theory, it faces the problem of accounting for the moral status of animals. Moreover, the assertion that moral agency confers special moral status is itself quite debatable. Consider both ways of supporting this assertion. The principle of reciprocity is put in doubt by the common-sense judgement that human babies have rights – for example, not to be abused – despite not being moral agents; and some babies will never become moral agents. Meanwhile, it is inconclusive to claim that the asserted connection between moral agency and rights is intuitively plausible. Many people find the assertion intuitively plausible, while many others, including me, do not. For those in the latter group, while moral agency is relevant to how one should be treated – since a moral agent must be treated as having certain responsibilities – it is irrelevant to how much, morally, one's interests matter.

The appeal to moral agency is probably strongest if detached from the dubious principle of reciprocity, since the latter entails that beings lacking moral agency have no moral status whatsoever. On the other hand, an appeal to moral agency that is not based on this principle might assert only that moral agents have *special* – not *exclusive* – moral status, allowing that sentient non-agents can have some degree of moral status. This position is less problematic than any view asserting that animals have no moral status. Still, if its only support is an appeal to intuitive plausibility, people's differing intuitions put this position in doubt. And this view problematically implies that some human beings have *less* moral status than others. We may reasonably conclude, then, that appeals to moral agency do not overturn the presumption of equal consideration.

Appeals to social bonds

A very different approach, developed by Mary Midgley, understands moral status as grounded in *relationships* rather than in an individual's characteristics, and appeals to the moral importance of *social bonds*. In our dealings with fellow humans, the argument begins, we recognize that how socially close we are to someone affects the strength of our obligations to that person. Thus, we have very strong obligations to our family members and closest friends and less strong obligations to other members of our various communities (for example, neighbourhood, school, religious group); our weakest obligations to other humans are those to complete strangers with whom we share no bond beyond membership in the human community. Still, the emotional and social bonds we feel for other humans count for something, grounding stronger obligations than we have to animals, with whom we form no special community. (Where there are exceptions, as in the case of companion animals, our obligations to the animals are quite strong.) Thus, the argument concludes, we may generally give less-than-equal consideration to animals.

This argument is correct that, in some respects, we have stronger obligations to those to whom we are especially close. For example, I have an obligation to provide for my child but no comparably strong obligation to provide for other children. But it is debatable what this suggests about equal consideration. After all, my *negative* obligations to other children have full force: I must not kidnap, abuse, or kill them regardless of how socially distant they may be from me. And while I have special *positive* obligations – obligations to provide certain goods – to my own child, I acknowledge that all children have the same basic rights as my child does; indeed, I would include certain positive rights, such as rights to adequate nutrition, clothing, and shelter and would not restrict this claim to children of my own nation or society. In this way, I extend equal consideration to all other children – and humans generally.

Additionally, just as equal consideration for all humans is compatible with somewhat different specific obligations towards different individuals, equal consideration for all sentient beings is compatible with different specific obligations to them. Thus, the common conviction that we have much stronger obligations to assist humans in distress than to assist animals in distress does not necessarily contradict equal consideration. After all, positive obligations are largely *discretionary* in the sense that we may choose whom to help amid the deafening cacophony of cries for assistance from around the world. That I choose to help famine-threatened Ethiopians rather than Salvadoran refugees in no way implies that I think the refugees deserve less-than-equal consideration. Similarly, that I give to human causes much more than I give to animal causes does not imply the judgement that animals deserve less-than-equal consideration.

Moreover, appealing to social bonds in an effort to defend unequal consideration is dangerous. For the reasoning that leads the inegalitarian to conclude that animals are not due equal consideration may, in some circumstances, offer no less justification to invidious forms of discrimination, such as racism. Imagine a community in which members of race X feel socially very bonded to each other but very distant from members of race Y. Taking social bonds to be the basis for moral status suggests that members of group X may rightly devalue the interests of members of group Y – and this is morally obnoxious.

In conclusion, where the present approach has ethically unpalatable implications it is problematic as a basis for moral status, and where it supports ethically sound conclusions it may be compatible with equal consideration. Perhaps this approach – understood as a challenge to equal consideration – can gain plausibility, however, with two moves. First, if we construe social bonds as *merely one factor in determining moral status*, rather than its sole determinant, there may be a way to avoid supporting invidious discrimination against some humans. Second, the idea that we have stronger positive obligations to other humans than we do to animals may be further developed. If all human beings have certain positive rights – including rights to food and shelter – then, even if *individuals* have discretion about which causes to support, some greater *collective* (perhaps represented by governments of wealthy countries or the United Nations) has obligations to endeavour to meet the needs in question. The basis of these obligations, the argument continues, is the notion of human community. Yet animals have no comparable positive rights to food or, even where weather conditions are life-threatening, shelter; and humans, whether considered individually or collectively, have no obligations to provide animals these goods. The next challenge to equal consideration picks up this argument.

Appeals to common-sense moral differences regarding assistance and killing

What may be the most powerful challenge to equal consideration appeals to two widely accepted differences between our obligations to humans and our obligations to animals. The first alleged difference is that all humans have certain positive rights that ground corresponding obligations of assistance, whereas animals lack such positive rights. The second alleged difference is that, ordinarily, it is morally worse to kill a human being than to kill an animal. To kill a bird gratuitously may be wrong and to kill a dog without cause may be even worse; but to kill a human without special justification (for example, self-defence) is far worse, indeed one of the worst things one can do. Even those who champion animal rights generally agree with these propositions about the comparative wrongness of killing humans and other animals. According to the present line of reasoning, these differences between humans and animals regarding obligations of assistance and the wrongness of killing are incompatible with equal consideration for animals.

In examining possible strategies for rebutting this challenge, here I can only mention a few lines of argument without entering into details. Beginning with the asserted difference regarding obligations of assistance, one might reply as follows. Assume, for the sake of argument, (1) that humans have positive rights that ground our obligations to assist humans in dire need and (2) that we have extremely limited, if any, obligations to assist animals in need. These differences, according to the rebuttal, are compatible with equal consideration. For suppose animals, like humans, have positive rights. We might understand the corresponding obligations along the lines of this principle: 'Make reasonable efforts to provide assistance *when assistance is likely to be genuinely helpful*'. But human interventions to help animals in need, the rebuttal continues, are generally just as likely to harm animals as to benefit them. Ecosystems are delicate and complex, easily disrupted by clumsy interventions. For example, if we intervene to save wolves from starvation by providing them food, that may lead to overpopulation and a new threat of starvation, as well as to wolves' overconsumption of animals on whom they prey. Thus, we usually do justice to wild animals by leaving them alone. Where interventions are likely to be helpful, they usually consist of interfering with animal-exploiting humans – say, by challenging sport hunters or whalers – and it is plausible to think people should sometimes intervene in this way. So this argument attempts to reconcile equal consideration with the judgement that, in practice, we should not extensively involve ourselves in assisting wild animals in need.

As for the alleged difference regarding killing humans and animals, there are two main strategies for rebuttal (which I have explored in detail elsewhere). The more common strategy is to argue that equal consideration does *not* imply equally strong moral presumptions against killing humans and animals. Equal consideration means that where an animal and human have comparable interests – say, in avoiding suffering – we must give equal moral weight to those interests. But although we use the same word, 'killing', to denote the taking of human and animal life, the beings' interests are not really comparable. A human's interest in remaining alive is, in normal circumstances, absolutely central to her welfare. Humans typically have life plans, projects, and deep personal relationships, all of which would be destroyed by untimely death. By contrast, assuming that it is in a dog's interest to remain alive (a claim supported in Chapter 4), it is reasonable to suppose that continued life is *less* central to the dog's welfare than it is to a human's welfare. Dogs have at most very truncated plans and, while they have relationships, they typically lack the depth and range that one finds in the typical human case. Thus, the argument continues, death is ordinarily less of a harm to a dog than it is to a human. When one compares humans to animals lower in the evolutionary tree, such as fish, the conviction that death harms a human more becomes almost irresistible.

While these comparative claims are intuitively plausible, it is difficult to provide a supporting theory that is both detailed and compelling. But, without such a theory, one may wonder whether the intuitive attractiveness of such claims stems from anything other than pro-human prejudice. An alternative approach, which Steve Sapontzis defends, is to deny that it is less morally problematic to kill sentient non-human animals than it is to kill humans. Both strategies attempt to show that there is nothing absurd or unreasonable about equal consideration for animals.

Conclusion: an unresolved issue

Whether or not animals are due equal consideration is an unresolved issue. I have defended a moral presumption in favour of equal consideration. Clearly, appeals to species will not overturn that presumption. Almost as certainly, contract theory will not do so either. But, while no published discussions of the appeals to moral agency and to social bonds have carried the burden of proof on the inegalitarian, it may be premature to preclude the possibility that the relevant arguments could be developed more successfully. Among the various challenges to equal consideration, the strategy of appealing to the common-sense moral differences regarding assistance and killing seems strongest. Combining this approach with either, or both, of the suitably developed appeals to moral agency and social bonds may offer the most formidable possible challenge to equal consideration. But the very real possibility that our intuitions regarding assistance and killing are shaped by pro-human, anti-animal prejudice justifies a continued presumption in favour of equal consideration. Only a challenge that was explicit, coherent, and more compelling than any produced so far could overturn that presumption.

An alternative view: the sliding-scale model

Suppose that the presumption favouring equal consideration for animals were successfully overturned. How, then, should we understand animals' moral status? As we have seen, the view that animals have no moral status is not plausible, in view of the arguments we have canvassed. But there is a position that falls in between that extreme one and the equal-consideration approach, a view that is intuitively fairly plausible and no doubt tacitly accepted by many people.

To get a handle on this view, one needs to imagine two particular scales and then merge them. The first is the phylogenetic scale, or at least one way of construing it. This scale is an evolutionary hierarchy with animal species that are more biologically and cognitively complex closer to the top. Thus, on this scale, humans are – currently!– atop the scale, with Great Apes and dolphins a bit lower (and hominids other than *Homo sapiens* in between, if we include extinct species). Elephants, gibbons, and monkeys, for example, would be somewhat lower on the scale, with canines and felines a bit lower, and rabbits and rodents lower still. Moving more quickly along the scale, mammals would generally be higher than birds, who are generally higher than reptiles and amphibians, who are generally higher than fish. For the most part, vertebrates – a class that includes all the taxa mentioned so far – would be higher than invertebrates. Invertebrates, of course, comprise an enormous variety of lifeforms, not all of which are sentient, although we cannot say with confidence where to draw the line between sentient and non-sentient animals. That, very crudely, is the first scale.

The second scale is a hierarchy of moral status. Beings at the very top have the highest moral status and deserve full consideration. Beings somewhat lower deserve very serious consideration but less than what the beings on top deserve. As one moves down this scale of moral status or moral consideration, the amount of consideration one owes to beings at a particular level decreases. At some point one reaches beings who deserve just a little consideration. Their interests have direct moral significance, but not much, so where their interests conflict with those of beings with much higher moral status, the former usually lose out. Right below the beings just described we may mentally draw a line. Any and all beings below this line have *no* moral status. If there is good reason to treat them with restraint, that is only because doing so is conducive to the interests of beings with moral status. This, then, is a scale of moral status, the sliding scale of unequal consideration.

To grasp the view under consideration – an alternative to equal consideration – merge the phylogenetic scale with the sliding scale of unequal consideration. In the resulting picture, humans alone enjoy full, equal consideration. Among existing species, Great Apes and dolphins are due a bit less consideration, elephants, gibbons, and monkeys a bit less, and so on and so forth. Right above the line between minimal and no moral status are the most primitive and cognitively simple sentient beings – almost certainly one or more invertebrate species. We may commonsensically assume that non-sentient beings have no interests, justifying the line above them. This view avoids the problems of the theory that animals lack moral status while easily accommodating the

Two frameworks for understanding animals' moral status

Equal-consideration framework

Animals deserve equal consideration (see box entitled 'Three increasingly strong senses of "animal rights"' on p. 20).

Sliding-scale model

Humans deserve full, equal consideration. Other animals deserve consideration in proportion to their cognitive, emotional, and social complexity. For example, a monkey's suffering matters less than a human's suffering but more than a rat's suffering, which matters more than a chicken's suffering.

common belief that killing a human is generally worse than killing a dog, which is generally worse than killing a bird, and so on. It also fits comfortably with the conviction that we have stronger positive obligations to humans than we do to other animals – since, on this view, we have stronger obligations to humans across the board.

The chief reason to reject this view is the presumption in favour of equal consideration. However intuitively appealing the sliding-scale model may be, we cannot responsibly accept it without an explicit, compelling justification for giving less-than-equal consideration to animals. Without such a justification, it is arbitrary in the extreme to discount the importance of, say, a dog's suffering just because the subject of suffering happens to be a dog. If it is right to discount or devalue an animal's interests across the board, there is some *reason* why this is right. And, to be sure there really is a reason, one had better find it. I strongly suspect, however, that there is no such reason to be found – and that is why I accept equal consideration.

Conclusion

This chapter has introduced the concepts of moral status, moral rights, and equal consideration and has presented leading arguments for and against attributing them to animals. Returning to the case with which the chapter began, we may now advance beyond the initial judgement that the cruel treatment of pigeons in the annual shooting festival was wrong. Why was it wrong? Because it caused extensive harm to animals for no compelling reason. But why is it wrong to cause pigeons or other sentient animals gratuitous harm? This is where the key concepts come into play.

First, pigeons and other sentient beings have *moral status*. That is, their interests – or, collectively, their welfare – have independent moral importance. In other words, we have obligations to animals, and these are obligations not simply grounded in human interests. Animals themselves can be wronged. We should treat animals well *for their sake*. Does this mean pigeons and other animals have *moral rights*? Yes, in at least the widest of the three senses of the term – according to which, to have moral rights is simply to have moral status.

Let us now consider the narrower, equal-consideration sense of 'rights'. The fact that the pigeons were treated wrongly does not entail that they are due equal consideration; causing gratuitous, extensive harm to birds would also count as wrong on the sliding-scale model, which grants moral status but not equal consideration to animals. If pigeons and other sentient beings are due equal consideration, then they have moral rights in this stricter sense. Equal consideration would rule out not only the pigeon hunts but also, for example, animal husbandry where people do not need the meat to survive (see Chapter 5). Suppose, on the other hand, the sliding-scale view is right. Then while it is wrong to shoot pigeons for fun, smash their heads, and suffocate them, it might not be wrong to give chickens fairly comfortable lives on family farms only to kill them for food – even though we don't really need to eat this meat and could not rightly use fellow humans in this way.

Do pigeons and other animals have rights in the strictest, utility-trumping sense? In this sense, one has a right to something, such as liberty of movement, only if others generally may not deprive one of that good even when doing so would maximize utility. For practical purposes, it is not so important to decide whether animals have rights in this utility-trumping sense (the context of animal research being a possible exception – see Chapter 7). The issues of moral status and equal consideration are far more fundamental and far-reaching in practical impact. Indeed, ethical theorists do not all agree that humans have rights in the utility-trumping sense. For these reasons, I have not explored the debate over animal rights in this sense, leaving that debate for professional philosophers.

Chapter 3
What animals are like

Cornered in the garage, the trembling racoon slowly backs up, focusing her eyes on the man who approaches with broom in hand. The man, who wants to chase the racoon out of the garage, sees the animal's behaviour as fearful. Her leg caught in a steel trap that has cut deep into the skin, a fox struggles for hours to free herself, to no avail, before slowly chewing off her leg and separating herself from the trap. A passerby who sees the fox just as she tears away from the trap – and her leg – perceives her as experiencing great pain and suffering. Staying at a kennel for the first time, as his human companion family takes a trip out of town, a dog is hypervigilant and jumpy, and urinates on the floor. The kennel worker assumes that the dog is anxious in this unfamiliar setting.

The attributions of fear to the racoon, pain and suffering to the fox, and even anxiety to the dog are natural enough, but are they well-grounded? Does available evidence support such interpretations of animals' behaviour? More generally, what sorts of mental lives do animals have? Although this question quickly leads into great complexity, both scientific and philosophical, this chapter offers only a preliminary and quite general discussion of the mental lives of animals – of what sorts of beings animals are, or what they are like. The chapter's central claim is that a wide range of animals, including most or all vertebrates and probably some invertebrates, possess a rich variety of

3. A fox caught in a leghold trap.

feelings. Before going to the evidence, though, we should clarify a few key terms.

Some basic concepts

To have any mental states or mental life at all, a being must have some *awareness* or *consciousness*. But what is awareness? We may elucidate the term by reference to other familiar terms and by use of examples.

A human or animal is aware at a particular time if he or she is having any subjective experiences at that time. Such experiences include all states of consciousness when we are awake and even those confused modes of thinking and feeling known as dream experiences. A closely related concept is that of *sentience* – the capacity to have *feelings*. Feelings, in turn, include both *felt sensations*, such as pain and nausea, and *emotional states*, such as fear and joy. All sentient beings have states of awareness. For example, presumably all sentient animals can feel at least painful and pleasant sensations.

It is important to distinguish awareness from *nociception*. Nociception, the first event in a sequence that often involves pain, is the detection of potentially noxious, or tissue-damaging, stimuli by specialized neural end-organs – nociceptors – which fire impulses along axons (nerve fibres that serve as pathways). Such stimuli include cutting, pressure, pricking, heat, cold, inflammation of tissues, and muscle spasms. While nociception itself is not a state of awareness or consciousness, it often occurs together with such states, typically pain. With Bernard Rollin, one might think of nociception as 'the machinery or plumbing of pain', although in atypical cases there can be nociception without pain – as when a severed spinal cord permits a paraplegic to retain a withdrawal reflex but prevents the occurrence of pain, or in an animal under general anaesthesia.

While there is no perfect definition of 'awareness', our experience and common sense are sufficient to understand this basic concept. Whenever we are awake or dreaming, we experience subjective states; and we know that, in certain sleeping states and under general anaesthesia, we have no such subjective states. As we will see, empirical evidence strongly supports the common-sense judgement that many animals also have states of awareness, even if their consciousness is less complex, reflective, and language-laden than human consciousness typically is.

Evidence for pain and other sensations in animals

Although nearly everyone believes that many animals experience pain, a responsible discussion of animal mentality must consider whether evidence supports this or any other attribution. But here, as with other mental states, we need a working definition to clarify what we are looking for. Our own experience – or phenomenology – of pain combined with scientific study of the phenomenon supports roughly this understanding: *pain is an unpleasant or aversive sensory experience typically associated with actual or potential tissue damage*. (This definition doesn't cover 'emotional pain', a figurative extension of the most literal sense of 'pain'; 'suffering' is often an apt and more literal substitute for 'emotional pain'.)

Now, when we ask whether a particular sort of creature experiences a type of mental state, four kinds of evidence are relevant. First, human phenomenology helps to categorize mental states and informs us of what they feel like. From this starting-point, which can help to establish a working definition, we can argue that non-human animals have a particular mental state on the strength of three other sources of information: animals' behaviour in context, their physiology, and functional-evolutionary considerations. The latter address the adaptive value of a type of mental state for a specific kind of creature living in a particular environmental niche.

Let us consider such evidence in connection with pain. Certainly, animals often behave as if in pain. Any of these three types of behaviour is at least somewhat suggestive of pain: (1) avoiding or escaping a noxious stimulus (for example, withdrawing a paw from a sharp object); (2) getting assistance (for example, crying out) after a noxious event; and (3) limiting the use of an overworked or injured body part to permit rest and healing (for example, immobilizing a pulled muscle and favouring another limb). The vast majority of animals, including insects, exhibit behaviours of type (1), though in some animals such behaviours may be due to nociception without pain or some similar type of non-conscious response to stimuli. Vertebrates and perhaps some invertebrates also display behaviours of type (3). Type (2), which may be relevant only to comparatively social animals, is common among mammals and birds. Evidence of learning and adaptation to novel circumstances strengthen the claim that behaviours of any of these three types indicate pain – and therefore sentience. Such evidence is found in the case of vertebrates and at least some invertebrate species such as octopuses and squid.

Turning now to physiological evidence for animal pain, there is extensive commonality across vertebrate species of the biological machinery apparently required for pain. Pain is associated with certain physiological changes, including measurable nerve impulses in specific pathways and metabolic and electrical activity in particular parts of the brain. In turn, these events elicit other physiological responses such as changes in the sympathetic adrenomedullary system and the hypothalamic-pituitary-adrenocortical system. Not only are the neurophysiology and neuroanatomy of pain quite similar in these animals; they also share the biological mechanisms for modulating pain, such as endogenous opiates. Moreover, anaesthesia and analgesia control what is apparently pain in all vertebrates and some invertebrates. Indeed, if animals were not significantly analogous to humans in the capacity for pain and other aversive mental states, it would be senseless to use animals as models for the study of these states in humans.

Consideration of pain's function in the context of evolutionary theory constitutes another form of evidence for animal pain. The biological function of pain is evidently (1) to provide an organism information about where tissue damage may occur, is occurring, or has occurred and (2) to motivate responses that are likely to avoid or minimize damage, such as rapid limb movement away from a noxious stimulus or immobilizing muscles to permit recuperation. Pain's unpleasantness provides the motivation for adaptive, life-preserving responses.

Then again, one might reply, perhaps nociception or some similar event – without pain or any conscious awareness – would function equally well to keep animals out of harm's way, in which case functional-evolutionary arguments might not support the case for animal pain. But evolution tends to preserve successful biological systems. And rather than spontaneously producing new creatures well-suited for particular niches, with no 'design constraints', evolution operates within the limits of the genetic endowment and anatomical systems inherited from evolutionary forebears. Now we know that in humans the ability to feel pain is important for functioning and survival. Humans with significantly impaired or no ability to feel pain, such as people with anaesthetic leprosy, are in danger of not surviving without extraordinary attention. The fact that neural structures similar to those that produce our consciousness are found in vertebrates – in combination with their pain behaviour – suggests that pain has a similar function for them and that natural selection has preserved the capacity for pain throughout the evolution of at least the vertebrates.

However, in all but the most 'advanced' invertebrates, such as octopuses and squids, there is genuine uncertainty regarding pain and, more generally, sentience. For example, the impressively complex behaviour of some insects, such as ants and bees, may seem to suggest sentience; one might take apparent pain behaviour in all insects – avoiding or escaping noxious stimuli – as strong evidence of pain in these creatures. Then again, some insect behaviour, such as continuing normal behaviour after injury or loss of body parts, and not taking weight off injured limbs, strongly suggests lack of sentience. Moreover, insects have extremely primitive nervous systems by comparison to vertebrates. Finally, with their short life spans and modest learning needs, insects might derive little advantage from conscious states such as pain; a startle reflex might suffice to enable escape from danger in most circumstances. Thus, the evidence available today is too indeterminate to justify confidently drawing the line between sentient and non-sentient animals in any specific place, although it is virtually certain that some invertebrates, such as amoebas, are non-sentient.

While there is much uncertainty regarding the possible sentience of invertebrates, as we have seen, evidence overwhelmingly supports the proposition that many animals, apparently including all vertebrates, can feel pain. But there is little doubt that animals who can feel pain can also feel pleasure – at least in the form of *pleasant sensations*. (That animals also experience pleasant *emotions* would require further arguments.) We may say the same of *bodily discomfort*, an unpleasant sensation distinct from pain. But here we cannot explore precise definitions or specific evidence for these mental states.

Evidence for distress, fear, anxiety, and suffering

While pain is sensory and therefore associated with specific body parts, distress, fear, anxiety, and suffering are emotional and therefore associated with the entire subject who experiences them. Before considering specific evidence for the occurrence of these states in animals, let us clarify the concepts themselves.

We may start with suffering, which has a sort of umbrella relationship to the others. Note that suffering differs from pain since either can occur without the other. If I pinch my hand, I have pain without suffering, whereas someone having a panic attack suffers without pain. Nor does suffering equal distress; if you are only mildly distressed due to a deadline, you do not suffer. *Suffering is a highly unpleasant emotional state associated with more-than-minimal pain or distress*. Since suffering is defined in terms of pain and distress, the evidence for suffering is the same as that for pain or distress – or high degrees thereof. Pain we discussed earlier.

Distress is a typically unpleasant emotional response to the perception of environmental challenges or to equilibrium-disrupting internal stimuli. It can be caused by such diverse phenomena as the sight of approaching predators, the belief that one will fail, or diarrhoea. Distress can take the form of various more specific mental states, such as fear, anxiety, frustration, and boredom. While a thorough exploration of distress would investigate all such related mental states, here we will consider just fear and anxiety.

Fear motivates focused responses to perceived dangers and preparation for future responses. While perhaps mild fear can be pleasant, as with skiing, fear tends to be unpleasant. *Fear is a typically unpleasant emotional response to a perceived danger (usually in the immediate environment), a response that focuses attention to facilitate protective action.* By contrast, anxiety involves a generalized, as opposed to focused, state of heightened arousal and attention to the environment. It usually immobilizes our mental resources and inhibits our action, so we can attend to our environment until we have determined how to respond to any challenges that may arise. While fear and anxiety are closely related, anxiety serves especially well in unfamiliar situations, explaining why it is less focused than fear. Moreover, at least with humans, often the object of anxiety is possible damage to one's self-image. *Anxiety is a typically unpleasant emotional response to a perceived threat to one's physical or psychological well-being, a response that generally inhibits action and involves heightened arousal and attention to the environment.* Commonsensically, fear and anxiety have similar protective functions in complementary settings. For example, a cat may be anxious in the novel setting of a veterinarian's waiting room. In her second visit there, she may feel fear due to remembering a painful shot she received during the previous visit. But let us move beyond common-sense claims to rigorous evidence.

Consider the evidence for anxiety, which of the mental states under discussion is most likely to inspire scepticism. First, typical behavioural and physiological features of human anxiety are also found in many animals in circumstances that are likely to make animals anxious, if any would: (1) autonomic hyperactivity – pounding heart, sweating, increased pulse rate and respiration, etc.; (2) motor tension, as seen in jumpiness; (3) inhibition of normal behaviours in novel situations; and (4) hyperattentiveness, as seen in visual scanning. Consistent with the definition of anxiety, these findings add up to strong behavioural evidence and some physiological evidence for anxiety in animals. In addition, we have already seen the adaptive value, or evolutionary function, of anxiety: it permits a creature to inhibit action and attend carefully to the environment in preparation for protective action.

Further, human anxiety and some mental states in animals – which we infer to be anxiety – are mediated in similar ways by certain drugs that cause similar neurophysiological and neurochemical changes. In one kind of test, for example, randomly punishing thirsty rats causes reduced drinking, the inhibition of a normal behaviour. But giving the rats an anti-anxiety drug restores drinking to more normal rates. Another kind of test places animals in novel settings such as brightly lit open spaces. Animals who are given anti-anxiety drugs beforehand exhibit what is apparently less anxious behaviour than animals who are not given these drugs. Moreover, when drugs that *induce* anxiety in humans are given to animal subjects, they display the behaviours and physiological responses associated with anxiety.

Since most of the subjects of these latter studies were mammals, the following findings are of special interest. Scientists have long known that benzodiazepine receptors, which in humans are the substrate for nearly all known anti-anxiety agents, are also found in mammals. More recent research demonstrated that none of the five invertebrates tested, nor the one cartilaginous fish (an animal at the border between vertebrates and invertebrates), had these receptors. Yet all the other species examined – including three species of birds, a lizard, frog, and turtle, and three species of bony fishes – had such receptors, providing some additional evidence that at least most vertebrates can experience anxiety.

While the available evidence, taken together, supports this conclusion, it does not imply that human anxiety and animal anxiety are qualitatively similar beyond a common unpleasantness and heightened arousal and attention. Undoubtedly, the language-laden complexity of human thought produces anxious experiences very different from those of animals. The present claim is that animals representing a wide range of species are capable of having anxious states, as captured in our definition of 'anxiety'.

Given the close relationship between anxiety and fear, as explained above, one would expect that animals capable of being anxious are also capable of being afraid. Supporting this common-sense judgement is the fact that all vertebrates have autonomic-nervous and limbic systems, which contain the basic substrates of fear and anxiety. And, of course, such animals often behave as if in fear – a state that has great adaptive value from an evolutionary standpoint.

But if certain animals can experience fear and anxiety – which are forms of distress – there is no further question of whether they can experience distress. Can they suffer, though? Suffering, again, is a highly unpleasant emotional state associated with more-than-minimal pain or distress. We have already argued that vertebrates can experience pain and distress. But if some animals can experience these states only *minimally* – that is, not very intensely – that would imply that they cannot suffer. It is unclear what would count as evidence that certain animals could have only minimal pain and distress, beyond the general speculation that the most primitive sentient creatures have dim mental lives. In any case, since apparently all vertebrates and at least some invertebrates are sentient, I recommend the tentative assumption that at least *most* vertebrates can suffer.

Responding to some sceptical arguments

The evidence we have considered supports the thesis that a wide range of animals, including most or all vertebrates and probably some invertebrates, possess a variety of feelings. It will not be possible, however, to discuss evidence for more sophisticated mental phenomena that animals may or may not share with humans – such as thinking or reasoning, language, and autonomous decision-making. (I have discussed these elsewhere.) But it will be worthwhile to identify and rebut several alleged grounds for scepticism about animals' mental lives.

One common contention is that animals lack awareness or consciousness because they lack *immortal souls*, conceived as immaterial substances. But this is an extremely weak argument. It ignores all the empirical evidence for animal awareness while resting on an assumption for which there is no evidence: that human beings but no other animals possess immortal souls. One wonders exactly when in hominid evolution our ancestors began to have souls! Indeed, developments in science and the philosophy of mind make it increasingly difficult – though certainly not impossible – to maintain that humans have immortal souls. Neurology and psychology find no explanatory value in positing such entities, while doing so introduces serious problems regarding causal relations between immaterial substances and material substances. Even if belief in a soul remains an important part of individual faith, such belief has no place in a responsible investigation of animals' mental lives.

Some philosophers have argued that because *language* is necessary for awareness, animals must lack awareness. Granting the implicit assumption that presently existing animals lack language – although a few highly trained Great Apes and dolphins may constitute exceptions – the argument remains unsound. While language is certainly necessary for verbal expression of one's states of awareness, there is no reason to think that language is always or even typically necessary for *having* those states. If it were, then human babies would be incapable of experiencing pain, pleasure, and fear before they acquired language – a notion whose implausibility is almost universally recognized today. It is true that some specific manifestations of feelings, such as fear *of one's own mortality*, involve such abstract thinking that they may require linguistic ability just to form the associated thoughts (for example, of mortality). But that in no way suggests that creatures lacking language have no feelings.

One also sometimes hears the claim that a high degree of *rationality* is necessary for states of awareness, including feelings. But there is no good reason to accept this claim. Certainly, a high degree of rationality is necessary for complex reasoning in response to certain feelings – such as devising elaborate plans for improving your health, thereby reducing the pain and distress caused by your illness. But to experience pain, distress, and other feelings we have discussed does not require sophisticated reasoning.

A sceptic might also attempt to challenge the thesis that animals have awareness by arguing that they lack *self-awareness*. But such an argument either fails to distinguish awareness and self-awareness or supposes that the former depends on the latter. But note that, conceptually, self-awareness is more specific and complex than basic awareness, involving the concept of a self. And, factually, there is no clear reason why all awareness must involve awareness of oneself. To see a tree requires awareness – assuming we use the term 'see' in a way that implies conscious experience – but this visual experience doesn't seem to require any conscious noting of who is doing the seeing. Thus, we typically think that even very young infants can have some feelings, such as painful and pleasant sensations, long before they achieve any significant form of self-awareness.

Then again, one might argue that, even if animals have some mental states, their lack of self-awareness entails that they lack some specified mental states such as suffering. Perhaps the previously stated definition of 'suffering' is incomplete; according to Eric Cassell, suffering involves a sense of oneself as existing over time and, in suffering, one feels a threat to the integrity of the self. While such sceptics tend to leave terms like 'integrity of the self' unhelpfully vague, let us grant the assumption that suffering involves a sense of oneself as existing over time – that is, *temporal self-awareness*.

4. A chimpanzee fishing for termites.

The chief difficulty with this case for scepticism about animal suffering is that there are very good reasons to think that many animals possess temporal self-awareness. Consider, for example, our assertion – which probably few people will deny – that vertebrates experience fear. Fear, I suggest, is impossible unless the subject has some awareness of persisting into the future. After all, one fears something that might happen to one – in the (possibly very near) future. One might, of course, preserve scepticism about temporal self-awareness, and suffering, in animals by insisting that they are incapable of fear. But we presented evidence for fear in animals and we have seen no evidence or arguments supporting the claim that animals lack temporal self-awareness.

Further considerations, including the following two, bolster the attribution of temporal self-awareness to many animals. First, the growing field of cognitive ethology – which examines animal behaviour in the context of evolutionary biology – tends to support the attribution of beliefs, desires, and intentional actions to many animals. The central claim is that the *best explanation* of their behaviour, given everything we know about them, requires these attributions. But if Rufus the dog wants (desires) to go outside to bury a bone, and intentionally does so, that suggests that Rufus has some awareness of himself as persisting over time; desires usually concern states of affairs involving oneself in the future, and intentions are carried out over time. Second, there is considerable independent evidence that vertebrate animals have memories as well as expectations for the future. For example, it has been rigorously demonstrated that many birds have extensive recall of where they have hidden food. Now if, as seems likely, any of an animal's memories or expectations include representations of *the animal herself*, as in a memory of being hurt, that would entail some temporal self-awareness. In conclusion, while suffering – along with certain other feelings, including fear – may require a degree of temporal self-awareness, there is a strong case that at least most vertebrates have such self-awareness.

Let us take stock. This chapter opened with three human observers, who attributed fear to a racoon, intense pain and suffering to a fox, and anxiety to a dog, respectively. Now we are in a position to say that available evidence often supports such attributions.

Chapter 4
The harms of suffering, confinement, and death

Having just moved into her new house, Rachel discovers a mouse in the cupboards. Concerned about animal welfare, she wants to remove the mouse as harmlessly as possible and considers two options. She can leave a lethal trap loaded with cheese; this product can be relied upon to kill a mouse instantaneously with a sudden crack of backbreaking metal. This option, Rachel figures, involves virtually painless death. Alternatively, she can use a 'humane' trap which, loaded with cheese, entices a mouse into a container that shuts when the cheese is disturbed; later, she can take the mouse in the container to a field and release her. Reflecting on these options, Rachel wonders whether painless death harms a sentient creature. If not, then painlessly killing a mouse would cause no harm. But why, she muses, does she believe the 'humane' trap is worth considering? After all, a captured mouse might remain in the trap for hours, while the homeowner is away at work or sleeping at night. During that time, and during transport to a field, the mouse will no doubt experience such unpleasant feelings as fear, anxiety, and frustration. When released in the field, the mouse may also feel sad at being separated from family or other social group members – if sadness is within the emotional repertoire of mice. Because the 'humane' trap would cause some experiential harm, it is clearly worse than the trap that kills instantaneously – unless death harms a mouse. In that case, the 'humane' trap would have the advantage of avoiding the harm of death.

A kangaroo has lived in comfortable captivity in a zoo for years. His distress at being separated from loved ones (at the time of capture) has largely passed. He no longer has hope of escaping from the zoo grounds. On the whole, dampened expectations have led to modest desires – for food, comfort, occasional stimulation, and the like – that are easily satisfied. If returned to the wild, this kangaroo would have much greater liberty but, on the whole, much more hardship as well – due to changing weather, the threat of disease (with no veterinarians around), and predators. His situation provokes questions about the value of liberty to an animal. Restrictions of liberty, especially severe ones, often harm animals – and humans – by causing them *distress and suffering*. But the kangaroo's captivity is not presently harmful in that way; let us even assume that the kangaroo would have lower experiential well-being or quality of life – and perhaps a shorter life expectancy – if he returned to the wild. Might he be better off anyway? In the wild, he would regain the opportunity to exercise his *natural capacities* – his sensory abilities, muscles, and 'wits' – more fully. He would reclaim a high degree of *species-typical functioning*, living more robustly the unique life of a kangaroo. Does that count for something, apart from effects on experiential well-being?

In general, what constitutes harm and benefit for animals? What are their major interests? Equivalently, what is the nature of animal well-being? Before addressing these questions, we needed to study animal minds to learn about the sorts of experiences animals can have, since *experiential* well-being is a major component of well-being. Now, before turning to specific ethical issues involving animals, we need to learn more about how our actions can affect their well-being.

The harm of suffering

Other things being equal, animals and humans are better off for having a high level of experiential well-being. Experiences that are pleasant, enjoyable, or attractive for the way they feel tend to make an individual well off. Primarily, such experiences are valued *intrinsically* or for their own sake; they feel good and we like them. But these experiences also have *instrumental* value, because one who feels good is usually better able to pursue aims or goals successfully. Individuals who feel bad are often distracted – by pain, fear, depression, etc. – from pursuing their usual aims; sometimes these aversive states are so distracting that they make an individual want only to put an end to them. (Of course, *intense* pleasure is also distracting. Maybe, then, there is an evolutionary basis for its tendency to be short-lived.)

Aversive mental states, then, are harms. For convenience, we might sacrifice a bit of precision and refer collectively to such states – pain, distress, fear, anxiety, suffering, etc. – simply as *suffering*. This will allow us to identify a type of harm with a single word. Suffering is a harm, and to cause another to suffer is to harm that individual. The most readily apparent way that humans harm animals is by causing them to suffer.

Just as pleasant mental states are intrinsically beneficial, suffering is intrinsically harmful. This point is not contradicted by the fact that sometimes it can be in one's interest to suffer. Someone guilty of terrible crimes may need to suffer in order to become truly repentant on the way to becoming a better person. One might benefit a cat by bringing her, kicking and miaowing, to the veterinarian's office for a procedure that restores functioning to her leg – even if the whole process entails some suffering. Moreover, each specific form of suffering (for example, fear, anxiety) has a biological function and therefore adaptive value, as we saw in Chapter 3. So while suffering is not always a harm, *all things considered*, it is always to some degree intrinsically harmful; no one is better off just for suffering. And, again, suffering is instrumentally harmful where it interferes with the pursuit of goals, aims, and projects. Humans characteristically have fairly elaborate life goals, whose achievement is very important to them. Animals have much less developed aims. Still, it makes sense to assume that even fish, for example, have some desires – such as to get food – and that suffering can interfere with such pursuits.

That suffering is a harm is not really controversial. Indeed, many people – including many animal researchers, policy-makers, and philosophers – assume that the *only* way we can harm animals is by causing them to suffer. Thus, it is commonly thought that painlessly killing an animal research subject is morally unproblematic because it causes no harm. Later we will see that this assumption is naïve.

The harm of confinement

Unlike plants, animals move around and do things; such mobile activity permits them, at a minimum, to secure the means of survival. *Sentient* animals experience feelings, such as pleasure and pain, in the course of their activity. Assuming that sentient animals have desires (as I have argued elsewhere), it makes sense to say that they *desire* to move about and do certain things. Moreover, when they are able to do what they want, they typically experience pleasure or satisfaction; when they are unable to do what they want, they typically experience frustration or other disagreeable feelings. Thus, liberty – the absence of external constraints on movement – is *generally* a benefit for sentient animals, permitting them to pursue what they want and need. Naturally, some restrictions of liberty are in an individual's interests – as with cribs – while other restrictions of liberty are at least compatible with one's interests – as with your neighbour's fence, which slightly restricts your movement.

Consider, by contrast, what we may call *confinement* – understanding the term narrowly as referring to *external constraints on movement that significantly interfere with one's ability to live well*. Confinement in this sense is harmful, by definition. Because prison significantly interferes with people's ability to live well, imprisonment is a form of punishment.

5. A tiger in a roadside menagerie.

Another clear example of confinement is forcing a monkey to live alone in a small, barren cage. Monkeys, after all, like to roam around, explore things, play, and spend time with other monkeys. Severe constraints on movement often cause pain and bodily discomfort – when living conditions are unnatural and prevent normal exercise – and nearly always cause distress and related unpleasant emotional experiences. In short, such external constraints normally induce suffering.

But are they ever harmful without causing suffering? Consider our zoo kangaroo, who is comfortable and whose experiential well-being would actually be lower in the wild: does captivity nevertheless harm him, to any degree? The answer to this question depends on the answer to an unresolved theoretical question: whether exercising one's natural capacities – or species-typical functioning – is intrinsically valuable (conducive to well-being independently of effects on experiential well-being). If so, then our comfortable kangaroo is to some degree harmed by remaining in the zoo, which severely limits his ability to exercise his natural capacities; on balance, he might be better off back in the wild, despite suffering more. If, on the other hand, liberty is valuable only to the extent that it promotes experiential well-being, then our kangaroo is clearly better off in comfortable captivity. While we cannot achieve a full appreciation of animal well-being without resolving this issue about the value of liberty, addressing most practical situations involving captivity need not await the outcome. Usually, captivity that significantly interferes with an animal's ability to exercise her capacities also causes her to suffer, entailing unambiguous harm.

Is death a harm?

Death is distinct from dying. Dying, a process involving a still-living individual, typically involves suffering, especially if the dying process is protracted. Suffering that may occur in dying is one reason to fear our own demise. But death itself precludes suffering along with all other experiences. It has no effect on experiential well-being except to end it. Is death a harm?

Our common-sense judgements suggest that death ordinarily harms human beings (at least postnatal human beings, foetuses being a controversial case). Perhaps death does not harm one who has lived very fully for ninety-five years. Surely death does not harm those who suffer pain they cannot bear, with no prospect for an improved quality of life. But *ordinarily*, we think, death harms the human being who dies, helping to explain why murder is such an atrocious crime. But *why* is death a harm in the case of human beings? And what does the answer imply about animals?

Some philosophers contend that death is a harm inasmuch as it thwarts a central *desire*: to stay alive. In normal circumstances, they argue, a human being cherishes her life *at least instrumentally – as a necessary means for the successful pursuit of more particular aims and projects*, such as raising children or finishing a book. Many people also value their lives *intrinsically*. Either way, they want – or desire – to live.

On this view, then, death harms only those individuals who desire to stay alive. This claim has far-reaching implications for animals, for probably very few animals possess even the *concept* of staying alive, much less the desire to do so. Suppose a house catches fire, with a dog inside. She is terribly frightened, no doubt sensing that she may soon be badly hurt or harmed. While her efforts to escape may serve to evade death, it is doubtful that she has the concepts of life and death, and the desire to live. On the present view, then, the dog would be harmed experientially by being burnt but would not be harmed by death itself.

A defender of the desire-based approach might argue that some individuals who lack a desire to stay alive are nevertheless harmed if death thwarts central desires they do have. Suppose a wolf wants to become the dominant member of his pack. He has formed some crucial alliances, has picked a few timely fights with wolves who were higher in the hierarchy but vulnerable, and is rising to the top. If he dies before reaching his goal, one might argue, death harms him by thwarting his desire to become the dominant group member – even if he lacks the concept of death. This innovation within the desire-based approach would significantly broaden the range of animals harmed by death. Still, it would include only those animals who have either (1) the concept of life and the desire to stay alive or (2) future-oriented projects.

Challenging all forms of the desire-based account of the harm of death is this example. A human baby is born in good health with loving parents who are fully prepared to care for her. At one week old, she is indisputably sentient and has the potential to develop the advanced cognitive life of a normal human being. As of now, however, she has no plans or projects, much less the concept of life. Suppose that, by some freak accident, the baby dies painlessly in her sleep. Desire-based accounts must judge that she is not thereby harmed. Yet, upon hearing such a story, many of us would consider it a tragedy – not just for the grief-stricken family members, but for the baby herself. The judgement that death harms the baby requires an alternative account of the harm of death.

Such an alternative – which Tom Regan, Steve Sapontzis, and I have defended – holds that *death is an instrumental harm in so far as it forecloses the valuable opportunities that continued life would afford*. Sentient beings can have valuable experiences, including those that enhance experiential well-being, such as pleasure and contentment, and perhaps also – depending on one's theory of well-being – any that involve exercising one's natural capacities. Death would rob the cat, or the human newborn, of the sort of life otherwise available to that individual, *even if he or she has no awareness of the opportunities in question*. On this view, then, one need not have sophisticated conceptual abilities or future-oriented projects to be harmed by death. Sentience alone would entail that one can have valuable experiences and that death would cut off such experiences. (Whether mere *potential* for sentience suffices to make death a harm is a further, debatable issue that is important in the abortion context.) On the other hand, if a creature has neither a desire for life nor future-oriented projects, and his future predictably holds in store experiences that are predominantly negative – that is, full of suffering – then the present account denies that death would harm that individual.

Now recall Rachel, who finds a mouse in her new abode. Learning of these two ways to think about death, she reasons as follows: 'The desire-based approach suggests that painless death wouldn't harm the mouse. The opportunities-based view suggests otherwise: if released in a field, the mouse would have the sorts of opportunities available in a mouse life. Death would foreclose these opportunities.' The opportunities-based view therefore makes sense of Rachel's judgement that the humane trap, which would entail some suffering but would preserve life, is well worth *considering*. Whether, in the end, she should use the humane trap depends on the perhaps more debatable judgement that the mouse's premature death would be a greater harm than the suffering entailed by use of the trap – some fear, frustration, and possibly sadness. But Rachel is pretty sure that death would constitute a harm.

She reflects further. Suppose a car hits her pet dog, breaking her leg. Rachel could either have the dog painlessly killed under anaesthesia, or have the leg set in a cast with a good chance for complete recovery. The second option would entail considerable soreness, frustration, and perhaps fear as the dog endures a cast for roughly one month. Yet, intuitively, Rachel thinks that not only she but her dog would lose something if the dog were painlessly killed. She reasons that this and similar judgements are better explained if we assume that the harm of death is a function of the opportunities it forecloses.

Are these harms comparable across species?

Like humans, animals can be harmed. They are clearly harmed by being caused to suffer. They are also harmed by confinement – restrictions of liberty that significantly interfere with their ability to live well. Whether restrictions of liberty that significantly interfere with species-typical functioning should count as confinement in this sense – and therefore as harmful – even where no suffering results, is debatable. So is the issue of which animals can be harmed by death: only those who desire to live, or also animals with future-oriented projects, or all sentient animals? The discussion above supports the more inclusive view, but the issue is hardly settled. In any case, a question arises with respect to the major types of harm we have considered. If a human and an animal are harmed in a particular way, should we regard the *magnitude* of the respective harms as comparable – roughly equal – or as significantly different? As we will see, the answers are important for understanding our moral obligations toward animals.

Since suffering is most fundamentally an experiential harm, it is reasonable to hold that if a human and an animal experience roughly equal amounts of suffering – however difficult, in particular cases, that may be to determine – they are comparably harmed. Of course, suffering is also instrumentally harmful, interfering with one's ability to pursue goals. But, by frustrating the pursuit of goals, suffering tends to breed further suffering – a point that applies to both humans and animals. Moreover, if species-typical functioning has value independently of experiential well-being, we must note that suffering can interfere with such functioning, for any animal. Overall, there is a strong case that a certain amount of suffering should count as a comparable harm, no matter what sorts of creatures the subjects are.

Is the harm of confinement comparable across species? Yes, to the extent that we understand this harm in terms of causing suffering, since we have found the harm of suffering to be comparable. But if restrictions of liberty can harm by interfering with species-typical functioning – even without causing suffering – then the harm of confinement includes that unique type of harm. While this point applies to all sentient animals, the claim that confinement may harm creatures to different degrees may prove justifiable, although this complexity is best explained in discussing the harm of death, to which we turn.

As we noted earlier, some people regard their continued existence as intrinsically valuable and therefore regard death as an intrinsic harm. Whether these judgements are correct is quite debatable. However, all agree that, ordinarily, death is *instrumentally* harmful in the case of humans. So let us focus on the instrumental harm of death. Is it comparable across species?

Many philosophers, including several major champions of animal rights, have answered negatively. Proponents of a desire-based view of the harm of death reason as follows: since most sentient animals have no desire for life – or, as the modified view would add, future-oriented projects – death doesn't harm those animals *at all*. So, obviously, death harms them less than it harms normal humans and any animals who meet the relevant criterion. Proponents of the opportunities-based account, which seems stronger, would argue along these lines: while death robs any sentient being of the opportunities available to her, the opportunities available to humans are more valuable than those available to significantly less complex creatures, including most or all animals. (To support this claim, some philosophers appeal to humans' allegedly superior capacities for enjoyment and satisfaction; others appeal to humans' allegedly more valuable characteristic activities and types of functioning.) Similarly, the opportunities available to monkeys are richer than those open to cats, which are greater than those available to seagulls, and so on – with differences in cognitive, emotional, and social complexity grounding such comparisons. In sum, the value of staying alive *to the individual living the life* varies across species, so the magnitude of the harm of death varies accordingly.

6. A broiler house.

To explore these issues of comparative value in depth would require plunging headlong into a quagmire of unresolved theoretical issues (which I have examined elsewhere). There is no significant consensus here. However, almost all commentators, including me, would accept this cautious claim: ordinarily, death harms human beings more than it harms members of a large class of sentient beings including at least those animals 'below' mammals. Similarly, one might argue, confinement impedes activities and functioning of greater value, or cuts off greater potential for enjoyment and satisfaction, in the case of humans than is the case of at least some animals, and to that extent harms humans more. We must remember, however, that major deprivations of liberty nearly always cause suffering – a harm that is comparable across species. (In principle, one could make a similar point about suffering *considered only instrumentally*: the types of functioning, or sources of satisfaction, it thwarts can differ in value across species. I will ignore this point, though, because suffering is primarily an experiential harm.)

Conclusions

Our discussion has yielded several conclusions. First, a certain amount of suffering is a comparable harm, regardless of who the sufferer is. Second, when comparing humans with some animals – at least those 'below' mammals – death is not a comparable harm. In normal circumstances, death harms humans more. Third, confinement is a comparable harm across species in terms of causing a certain amount of suffering; it is not comparable, when comparing humans and at least some animals, in terms of interfering with valuable activities or possibilities for satisfaction. Let us now briefly consider the potential ethical ramifications, by revisiting the ethical frameworks sketched in Chapter 2.

If one accepts an equal-consideration framework, one holds that we should give equal moral weight to humans' and animals' *comparable* interests. Thus, equal consideration implies that causing animals to suffer is as morally problematic as causing humans to suffer. As we will find in later chapters, many institutions of animal use dramatically fail to meet this standard. On the other hand, it is consistent with equal consideration to hold that, regarding a wide range of animals, the moral presumption against killing humans is stronger than that against killing those animals. (This claim receives further support from other considerations, including the greater emotional harm that loved ones typically experience when a human dies.) And, in the case of such animals, the moral presumption against confining them is *somewhat* weaker than the presumption against confining humans.

Rejecting equal consideration, the inegalitarian would pay somewhat less attention to subtle claims about comparable and incomparable harms. She judges that human interests are morally weightier than animals' interests *across the board*. And, in general, the greater an animal's cognitive, emotional, and social complexity, the more weight the animal's interests should receive, justifying a hierarchy or sliding scale of unequal consideration across species. Claims of incomparability regarding, say, the harm of death may lead the inegalitarian to judge that, in the case of many animals, there is very little presumption against painlessly killing them – say, in biomedical research. Perhaps more importantly, the inegalitarian denies that causing suffering is equally morally problematic in the case of frogs, thrushes, rats, and humans – even if we should never be cavalier about causing suffering to anyone.

Having now explored the moral status of animals, their mental lives, and major ways in which they can be harmed, let us turn to practical ethical issues concerning the human use of animals.

Chapter 5
Meat-eating

Hen X begins life in a crowded incubator. She is taken to a 'battery' cage made entirely of wire – and quite unlike the outdoor conditions that are natural for her – where she will live her life. (Having no commercial value, male chicks are gassed, ground up alive, or suffocated.) Hen X's cage is so crowded that she cannot fully stretch her wings. Although her beak is important for feeding, exploring, and preening, part of it has been cut off, through sensitive tissue, in order to limit the damage caused by pecking cage mates – a behaviour induced by overcrowding. For hours before laying an egg, Hen X paces anxiously among the crowd, instinctively seeking a nest that she will not find. At egg-laying time, she stands on a sloped, uncomfortable wire floor that precludes such instinctual behaviours as pecking for food, dust bathing, and scratching. Lack of exercise, unnatural conditions, and demands for extreme productivity – she will lay 250 eggs this year – cause bone weakness. (Unlike many hens, Hen X is not subjected to forced moulting, in which water is withheld one to three days and food for up to two weeks in order to extend hens' productive lives.) When considered spent at age 2, she is jammed into a crate and transported in a truck – without food, water, or protection from the elements – to a slaughterhouse; rough handling causes several weak bones to break. At her destination, Hen X is shackled upside down on a conveyor belt before an automated knife slices her throat. Because the (US) Humane Slaughter Act does not apply to poultry, she is fully conscious throughout this process. Her body, which was extensively damaged during her lifetime, is suitable only for pot pies, soup, and the like.

After weaning at four weeks of age, Hog Y is taken to a very crowded, stacked nursery cage. Due to poor ventilation, he breathes in powerful fumes from urine and faeces. Upon reaching a weight of 50 pounds, he is taken to a tiny 'finishing' pen. It is slatted and has a concrete floor with no straw bedding or sources of amusement. Despite being a member of a highly intelligent and social species, Hog Y is separated from other hogs by iron bars and has nothing to do except get up, lie down, eat, and sleep. He sometimes amuses himself by biting a tail in the next crate – until all the hogs' tails are 'docked' (cut off). Both this procedure and castration are performed without anaesthesia. When he is deemed ready for slaughter, Hog Y is roughly herded into a truck with thirty other hogs. The two-day journey is not pleasant for Hog Y, who gets in fights with other hogs while receiving no food, water, rest, or protection from the summer heat. At the slaughterhouse, Hog Y smells blood and resists prodding from the human handlers. They respond by kicking him and smashing him repeatedly from behind with an iron pipe until he is on the restraining conveyor belt that carries him to the stunner. Hog Y is fortunate in so far as the electric stunning procedure is successful, killing him before his body is dropped in scalding water and dismembered. (Although the Humane Slaughter Act requires that animals other than poultry be rendered unconscious with a single application of an effective stunning device before being shackled, hoisted upside down, and dismembered, many slaughterhouse employees state that violations occur regularly. Fearing that a higher voltage might cause 'bloodsplash' in some carcasses, many slaughterhouse supervisors apparently encourage use of a voltage that is much too low to ensure unconsciousness. Moreover, in numerous slaughterhouses stunners have to stun an animal every few seconds and face extreme pressure not to stop the line of animals.)

Although it is natural for cows and their calves to bond strongly, Cow

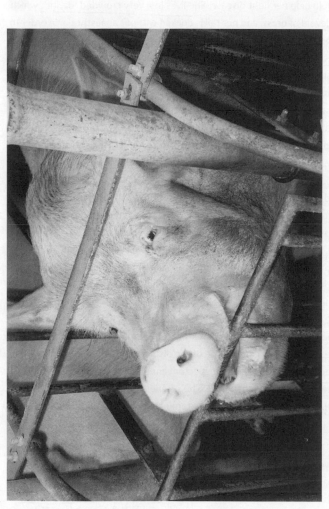

7. A pig chewing on a bar.

(then Calf) Z is taken from her mother shortly after birth to begin life as a dairy cow. She never receives colostrum – her mother's milk – which would help her fight disease. She lives in a very crowded 'drylot', which is devoid of grass, and her tail is docked without anaesthesia. In order to produce twenty times more milk than a calf would need, she receives a diet heavy in grain – not the roughage that cows have evolved to digest easily – causing metabolic disorders and painful lameness. And like many dairy cows, she often has mastitis, a painful udder inflammation, despite receiving antibiotics between lactations. To maintain continuous milk production, Cow Z is induced to bear one calf each year. To stimulate additional growth and productivity, she receives daily injections of bovine growth hormone. Her natural life span is twenty or more years, but at age 4 she can no longer maintain production levels and is deemed 'spent'. During transport and handling, Cow Z is fortunate: although deprived of food, water, and rest for over two days, and frightened when prodded, she is not beaten; at the slaughterhouse her instincts – unlike hogs' – allow her to walk easily in a single-file chute. Unfortunately, the poorly trained stun operator has difficulty with the air-powered knocking gun. Although he stuns Cow Z four times, she stands up and bellows. The line does not stop, however, so she is hoisted up on the overhead rail and transported to the 'sticker', who cuts her throat to bleed her out. She remains conscious as she bleeds and experiences some of the dismemberment and skinning process alive. (The federal inspector cannot see what is happening where he is stationed; besides, he's frenetically checking carcasses that whiz by, for obvious signs of contamination.) Cow Z's body will be used for processed beef or hamburger.

The institution of factory farming

The animals portrayed above offer examples of life in modern factory farms, which now supply most of our meat and dairy products in the USA, Great Britain, and most other industrial countries. Since the Second World War, factory farms – which try to raise as many animals as possible in very limited space in order to maximize profits – have driven three million American family farms out of business; over the same time period, Great Britain and other nations have witnessed similar transformations in their agricultural sectors. Scientific developments that have fuelled the emergence of factory farming include the artificial provision of vitamin D (which otherwise requires sunlight for its synthesis), the success of antibiotics in minimizing the spread of certain diseases, and advanced methods of genetic selection for production traits. Since the driving force behind this institution is economic efficiency, factory farming treats animals simply as means to this end – as mere objects with no independent moral importance, or moral status, whatever.

Considering both numbers of animals involved and the extent to which they are harmed, *factory farming causes more harm to animals than does any other human institution or practice*. In the USA alone, this institution kills over 100 million mammals and five billion birds annually. American farm animals have virtually no legal protections. The most important applicable federal legislation is the Humane Slaughter Act, which does not cover poultry – most of the animals consumed – and has no bearing on living conditions, transport, or handling. Moreover, as Gail Eisnitz and others have extensively documented, the Act is rarely enforced. Apparently, the US Department of Agriculture supports the major goal of agribusiness: absolute maximization of profit without hindrance. This is not surprising when one considers that, since the 1980s, most top officials at USDA either have been agribusiness leaders themselves or have had close political and financial ties to the industry.

By contrast, European nations have curbed some of the excesses typified by American factory farming. For example, Great Britain has banned veal crates and limits to fifteen hours the amount of time animals can go without food and water during transport. The European Community and the Council of Europe have developed requirements for the well-being of farm animals that are translated into law in different member nations. These requirements generally provide animals with more space, greater freedom to engage in species-typical behaviours, and more humane living conditions than those of farm animals in the USA. Despite the more humane conditions that are typical in Europe, however, most European animal husbandry remains sufficiently intensive to merit the term 'factory farming'.

So far this discussion has provided a descriptive sense of factory farms primarily through three cases. Therefore it might be objected that the situations of Hen X, Hog Y, and Cow Z do not represent universal features of factory farming. That is correct. But the experiences of these three animals, the evidence suggests, are not atypical – at least in the USA. Still, while a thorough description of factory farms is impossible here, it may be helpful to add a few general remarks about other types of farm animals. The following generalizations are meant to describe the American situation, although some of them accurately describe the experiences of animals in many other countries as well.

Cattle raised specifically for beef are generally better off than the other animals described here. Many have the opportunity to roam outdoors for about six months. After that, they are transported long distances to feedlots, where they are fed grain rather than grass. Major sources of pain or distress include constant exposure to the elements, branding, dehorning, unanaesthetized castration, the cutting of ears for identification purposes, and a sterile, unchanging environment. We may add, of course, the harms associated with transportation to the slaughterhouse and what takes place therein.

Broiler chickens spend their lives in enclosed sheds that become increasingly crowded as tens of thousands of birds grow at an abnormally fast rate. Besides extreme crowding, major sources of concern include cannibalism, suffocation due to panic-driven piling on top of one another, debeaking, and very unhealthful breathing conditions produced by never-cleaned droppings and poor ventilation.

Veal calves' deprivations are similar to many of those that hogs experience. Formula-fed veal calves in particular live in solitary crates too small to permit them to turn around or sleep in a natural position. Denied water and solid food, they drink a liquid milk replacer deficient in iron – making possible the gourmet white flesh and resulting in anaemia. This diet and solitary confinement lead to numerous health problems and neurotic behaviours.

Let us now consider the overall picture: *factory farming routinely causes animals massive harm in the form of suffering, confinement, and death.* Regarding suffering – or experiential harm in general – all evidence suggests that factory farm animals, in the course of their lives, typically experience considerable pain, discomfort, boredom, fear, anxiety, and possibly other unpleasant feelings. (See Chapter 3 for a discussion of animals' mental lives.) Furthermore, factory farms by their very nature *confine* animals in our stipulated sense of the term; that is, they impose external constraints on movement that significantly interfere with living well. (For at least part of their lives, cattle raised specifically for beef are not confined in this sense.) And, of course, factory farming ultimately kills animals raised for meat, adding the harm of death – assuming, as argued in Chapter 4, that death harms such beings as cows, pigs, and chickens. Then again, death counts as a harm here only if we consider the sorts of lives these animals *could* have under humane treatment. Given animals' current treatment, death would seem to be a blessing, except possibly in the case of beef cattle. In any event, the general thesis that factory farms cause massive harm to animals is undeniable.

Moral evaluation

If the first crucial insight in a moral evaluation of factory farms is that they cause massive harm to animals, the second crucial insight is this: *consumers do not need the products of factory farms.* We cannot plausibly regard any of the harms caused to these animals as *necessary*. Unusual circumstances aside – say, where one is starving and lacks alternatives – we do not need to eat meat to survive or even to be healthy. The chief benefits of meat-eating to consumers are *pleasure*, since meat tastes especially good to many people, and *convenience*, since switching to and maintaining a vegetarian diet requires some effort. Putting the two key insights together brings us to the conclusion that *factory farms cause massive unnecessary harm*. Since causing massive unnecessary harm is wrong if *anything* is wrong, the judgement that factory farming is an indefensible institution seems inescapable.

Note that this condemnation of factory farming does not depend on the controversial assumption that animals deserve equal consideration. Even if one accepts a sliding-scale model of moral status, which justifies less-than-equal consideration for animals, one cannot plausibly defend the causing of massive unnecessary harm. Thus, it appears that if one takes animals at all seriously – regarding them as beings with at least some moral status – one must find factory farming indefensible.

But what about the consumer? She isn't harming animals; she's just eating the products of factory farming. Well, imagine someone who says, 'I'm not kicking dogs to death. I'm just paying someone else to do it.' We would judge this person to act wrongly for encouraging and commissioning acts of cruelty. Similarly, while meat-eaters may typically feel distant from meat production, and may never even think about what goes on in factory farms and slaughterhouses, the purchase of factory-farmed meat directly encourages and makes possible the associated cruelties – so the consumer is significantly responsible. In general, the following moral rule, although somewhat vague, is defensible: *make every reasonable effort not to provide financial support to institutions that cause extensive unnecessary harm.*

By financially supporting massive unnecessary harm, the purchase of factory-farmed meat violates this principle and is therefore, I argue, morally indefensible. Interestingly, we reached this important conclusion without commitment to any specific ethical theory such as utilitarianism or a strong animal-rights view. In any event, while our case against factory farming and buying its products has so far cited considerations of animal welfare, it is further strengthened by considerations of human welfare. How so?

First, animal products – which are high in fat and protein and contain cholesterol – are associated with higher levels of heart disease, obesity, stroke, osteoporosis, diabetes, and certain cancers. Medical authorities now recommend much less meat and more grains, fruits, and vegetables than Americans, for example, typically consume. Second, American factory farming has driven three million family farms out of business since the Second World War, as huge agribusinesses, enjoying billions of dollars in annual government subsidies, have increasingly dominated; while American consumers frequently hear that factory farming lowers meat prices at the cash register, they are rarely reminded of the hidden cost of tax subsidies. In Britain and many other countries, relatively few large agribusinesses have similarly come to dominate, putting many smaller farms out of business. Third, factory farming is devastating for the environment. It excessively consumes energy, soil, and water while causing erosion of topsoil, destruction of wildlife habitat, deforestation, and water pollution from manure, pesticides, and other chemicals. Fourth, factory farming has a perverse effect on the distribution of food to humans. For example, it takes about 8 pounds of protein in hog feed to generate one pound of pork for humans and 21 pounds of protein in calf feed to yield 1 pound of beef. Consequently, most US-produced grain, for example, goes to livestock. Unfortunately, wealthy countries' demand for meat makes plant proteins too costly for the masses in the poorest countries. Poor communities often abandon sustainable farming practices to export cash crops and meat, but profits are short-lived as marginal lands erode, causing poverty and malnutrition. There is, in fact, easily enough grain protein, if used sensibly, to feed every human on Earth. Fifth, perhaps especially in the USA, factory farming is cruel to its employees. It subjects them to extreme work pressures – as seen in a worker who cuts up to ninety chickens per minute, or urinates on the workline for fear of leaving it – and to some of the worst health hazards faced by any American workers (for example, skin diseases, respiratory problems, crippling hand and arm injuries, injury from wild, improperly stunned animals) – all for low pay. Finally, deregulation of the American meat industry since the 1980s, combined with extremely fast production lines, have made it virtually impossible to ensure safe meat. As noted by Henry Spira (see Singer's book on Spira), it has been estimated that contaminated chicken, for example, kills 2,000 Americans a year.

Thus, receiving further support from considerations of human welfare, the case for boycotting factory farm products is extremely powerful. But let us not ignore the following important objection. One might argue that the continuation of factory farming is economically necessary. Putting this industry out of business – say, through a successful boycott – would obviously be devastating for agribusiness owners, but would also eliminate many jobs and possibly harm local economies. These consequences, the argument continues, are unacceptable. Thus, just as factory farming is necessary, so is the extensive harm it inevitably causes to animals – contrary to my charge of massive *unnecessary* harm.

In reply, we may accept the factual assumption about likely consequences while rejecting the claim that they are unacceptable. First, as Peter Singer notes, the negative costs of ending factory farming would have to be borne only once, whereas perpetuating this institution entails that the costs to animals continue indefinitely. Also, considering how badly factory farm employees are treated, it is hard to believe they would be seriously harmed by having to seek alternative employment, as innumerable 'burnt out' employees do anyway. More generally, the various threats to human well-being posed by factory farming – health risks, environmental destruction, inefficient use and perverse distribution of grain proteins, etc. – could be avoided if this industry is eliminated (assuming it is not simply replaced by less intensive animal husbandry, which would perpetuate some of these problems). Avoiding these risks and harms, not once but indefinitely, would seem to counterbalance any short-term economic harm. Finally, I submit that *there are moral limits to what we may do to others in the pursuit of profit or employment – and causing sentient beings massive harm in pursuing these goals oversteps those bounds.* (Cases in which people are forced into prostitution, pornography, or slavery vividly exemplify the violation of such limits.) If that is correct, then factory farming cannot be considered necessary. In conclusion, I suggest that these rebuttals, taken together, undercut the argument from economic necessity.

Traditional family farming

This chapter has focused on factory farms because most of the animal products we consume come from this source. But people also eat animals from other sources, including traditional family farms.

Because they involve far less intensive rearing conditions, family farms cause much less suffering to animals than factory farms do. Family farms may not even confine animals in our sense of imposing constraints on movement that significantly interfere with living well. But, assuming the opportunities-based account of the harm of death is correct (see Chapter 4), farm animals cannot fully escape harm because they are ultimately killed, entailing the harm of death.

Causing much less harm to animals, and avoiding at least some threats that factory farming poses to human well-being (for example, water pollution, extremely hazardous working conditions), family farming is much more defensible than its dominant competitor. Still, there is a strong moral case against family farming and the practice of buying its products. For one thing, this institution does impose some significant suffering through certain practices: branding and dehorning cattle;

castrating cattle and hogs; separating mothers from offspring, which may well cause distress even to birds; and treating animals roughly in transport, handling, and slaughter. And, again, all the animals die. Since meat-eating is – unusual circumstances aside – unnecessary, these harms are unnecessary. It is difficult to defend the routine imposition of unnecessary harm.

A few possible replies, however, may strengthen the case for some forms of family farming. For example, chickens and turkeys can escape most of the harms just described. If a chicken or turkey is able to live a pleasant life – say, with family intact – and is never abused, the only relevant harm would be death. But one who defends a desire-based account of the harm of death (despite my critique in Chapter 4) would probably deny that birds are even subject to this harm, suggesting that in optimal conditions poultry are not harmed at all.

Alternatively, if one (unlike the present author) accepts the sliding-scale model of moral status, one would grant unequal moral weight to the interests – including the avoidance of suffering – of different beings depending on their cognitive, emotional, and social complexity. Perhaps proponents of this ethical framework would defend practices of family farming that keep the admittedly unnecessary suffering to a minimum. They might argue that it is not always wrong to cause *minimal* unnecessary harm, even to mammals, especially if there are some significant benefits such as employment for farmers. Then again, one would need to consider negative effects on human welfare, such as extremely inefficient use of grain protein, in assessing the plausibility of this line of argument.

Seafood

Much of the meat we consume comes from the sea. Beginning with fish and cephalopods (octopuses and squid), we concluded in Chapter 3 that these creatures are sentient, subject to pain and distress; we left somewhat more open whether they can experience suffering in the specific sense: a highly unpleasant emotional state associated with more-than-minimal pain or distress. Now catching fish and cephalopods requires hooking or netting them and causing them to suffocate. Clearly, they experience unpleasant feelings in the process. While traditional fishing methods do not involve confinement – since the animals are at liberty in their natural environment – death is obviously unavoidable. Death harms such creatures *to some degree* on the opportunities-based account of the harm of death, but not on the desire-based view.

There are several ways in which one might argue that fish and cephalopods are harmed only minimally: by claiming that any suffering is very brief; by denying that they suffer at all; or by arguing that the harm of death in their case is negligible to non-existent. Then one might argue that this minimal harm is adequately counterbalanced by certain benefits to humans: pleasure, convenience, rounding out a healthful diet, and employment for fishers. (One who believes that animals have rights in the strongest, utility-trumping sense – see Chapter 2 – would reject such reasoning, however.) Naturally, a proponent of the sliding-scale model of moral status will find the production and consumption of seafood easier to defend, since fish and cephalopods would be relatively low in the moral hierarchy.

One complicating factor in our analysis is that many fish today are raised in fish farms. These are so crowded that they amount to confinement and increase the unpleasantness of the fish's lives. When fish are raised in this way, the case for boycotting these products is stronger.

What about lobsters, crabs, shrimp, and other invertebrates other than cephalopods? Available evidence leaves open the issue of their possible sentience. If they are not sentient, our actions cannot harm them. People might reasonably disagree about whether, in this state of uncertainty, we should give them the benefit of the doubt and assume they are sentient.

As we think about the issue of eating seafood, we must not ignore any harms caused to creatures other than those consumed. For example, suppose you buy tuna fish from a company whose nets often ensnare and kill dolphins – whose cognitive, emotional, and social complexity rivals that of Great Apes. The harms thereby caused to dolphins might make the purchase of tuna from this company as serious a moral matter as buying meat from factory farms.

Chapter 6
Keeping pets and zoo animals

Jenny, a 5-year-old golden retriever, lives comfortably. She eats well, receives veterinary care when necessary, and is free from abuse. But she spends much of her time bored and alone. Twice a day she enjoys fifteen-minute walks on a leash. The house where she lives has a large backyard but it is not fenced in, so she gets outside only during walks. Both human parents work away from home during the day. Their one child is affectionate towards Jenny but interacts with her only sporadically, and is away most of the day.

Two lions, Leo and Leona, are the sole occupants of a zoo exhibit. They were bred at two different zoos, separated from their mothers after weaning, and brought together at the present zoo, where they gradually became accustomed to each other. Leo and Leona live comfortably in their medium-sized exhibit, most of which is outdoors. They eat well and receive good veterinary attention. But they are bored and listless, and they interact little with each other. By contrast with wild lions, who spend much of their time hunting for food, Leo and Leona never hunt for food or in other ways fully engage their senses, muscles, or intelligence. They seldom play.

Both scenarios depict animals whose liberty or freedom of movement has been restricted by human intervention. Is it ever right to restrict animals' liberty? If so, under what conditions? Is captivity necessarily harmful for animals, or disrespectful towards them? This chapter explores these and related questions.

Conditions for keeping animals

In my view, human companions and caretakers must satisfy two conditions to justify the keeping of particular animals. First, *the animal's basic physical and psychological needs must be met*. This basic-needs requirement can be defended by appealing to basic decency on the assumption (defended in Chapter 2) that animals have moral status. It receives further support from the idea that, in taking on a pet or zoo animal, one assumes responsibility for the animal's well-being. Hence the judgement that someone who lets his cat starve cannot get off the hook by pointing out that he did not actively harm the cat; special positive obligations flow from special relationships where one assumes the care-taking role.

Second, *the animal must be provided with a life that is at least as good as she would likely have in the wild*. This comparable-life requirement receives support from the plausible claim that we should not make animals worse off for being pets or zoo animals, since making them worse off would constitute *unnecessary harm*.

But, one may ask, isn't keeping animals sometimes *necessary* – say, to preserve a species, or to provide a blind person with a seeing-eye dog? If so, then any harms entailed by keeping animals in such cases are also necessary. Yet we must address such claims of necessity case-by-case. The 'necessity' is always relative to some goal, such as species preservation, the importance of which we must assess before determining whether pursuing the goal justifies harming anyone. (Strong animal-rights views would, as a matter of principle, reject harming some individuals, without their consent, to promote others' interests.) If a particular case of harming an animal – say, harshly training a dog to assist the blind – strikes one as *obviously* necessary, that may be because one tacitly assumes that the animal has inferior moral status and is rightly subordinated to human needs.

In any case, one can defend the comparable-life requirement in another way. Surely it would be wrong to permit a couple to adopt a child, if we knew she would thereby become worse off – say, because the foster home is benign and the couple are highly abusive. Equal consideration, then, requires the same standard for animals: not making them worse off for being pets or zoo animals. Naturally, those who reject equal consideration in favour of the sliding-scale model would not accept this second argument for the comparable-life condition. As for the first argument, based on the charge of unnecessary harm, they might either (1) consider a wider range of cases to fall under the category of 'necessary' harm or (2) challenge the idea that it is always wrong to harm animals unnecessarily. Thus, supporters of the sliding-scale model might accept only the basic-needs condition as a *requirement*, classifying the comparable-life condition as a moral *ideal* whose achievement is discretionary.

If I am correct that both conditions are genuine requirements, how do they relate? Where one is lax, the other picks up ethical slack. If your pet dog would truly languish in the wild, as a stray, you might be able to meet the comparable-life condition without meeting, say, his needs for adequate stimulation, exercise, and contact with other dogs. But the basic-needs requirement would not permit such neglect. If the basic needs of a zoo's groundhogs are met, but barely, while they would likely flourish in the wild, then the comparable-life condition finds fault with keeping them in present conditions.

Accepting these or similar requirements should help to avoid certain overgeneralizations – for example, that zoo exhibits are intrinsically harmful, or necessarily violate some right of animals. Some leading critics of zoos, including Dale Jamieson and Tom Regan, do not distinguish between *captivity*, which restricts one's liberty, and *confinement* in our specific sense: restricting liberty *in a way that significantly interferes with one's ability to live well*. The distinction is important because only confinement entails harm. Indeed, sometimes captivity or some other restriction of liberty is, on balance, beneficial. After all, one may have *liberty* – lack of external constraints – yet not enjoy certain important *freedoms*. A child using the internet, or a prey animal, may have liberty yet not be free from predators.

If captivity does not always harm animals, is it nevertheless *disrespectful*? In virtually every case of captivity animals are, at least in part, *used for human purposes*, such as enjoyment (zoo animals) and companionship (pets). Perhaps respect requires leaving animals alone in the wild and not producing animals for domestication. Some critics have argued that we should stop captive breeding of zoo animals and pets, let existing ones live out their lives without replacing them, and permit fully domesticated species to go extinct.

This view is unpersuasive. It is true that, in the case of normal, mature human beings we affirm a principle of *respect for autonomy* that requires their informed consent for interventions that use them for societal benefit (say, in research) and even for many interventions that benefit them (say, in medicine). But this principle applies to beings who have a substantial understanding of their own best interests and values; it does not apply to young children or non-human animals, who – with *very* few possible exceptions, such as language-trained apes – lack the reasoning and decision-making capacities that constitute *autonomy*. So it is appropriate to make decisions, on behalf of young children and animals, that accord with their interests. No one has ever cogently defended a principle of respect that applies to all sentient non-human animals and requires that we simply leave them alone.

Since keeping pets and zoo animals is neither intrinsically harmful nor necessarily disrespectful, we must assess the appropriateness of doing so with attention to the details of particular cases.

Pets

Returning to Jenny the golden retriever, her human companions have clearly not satisfied both conditions for keeping animals. Admittedly, if Jenny became a stray, she would probably be worse off. While gaining a more exciting life, she would be hungry much of the time, would lack veterinary care, and would be subject to weather extremes and miscellaneous outdoor dangers. So let us assume the comparable-life condition is met: Jenny's life is certainly no less good, on balance, than it would be if she were a stray. But her human companions have violated the basic-needs condition by failing to meet her needs for ample exercise, stimulation, and companionship.

Since Jenny's situation is not unusual for a pet, it is worth asking how her human companions could meet the basic-needs condition. First, they could significantly increase the amount of time she is outside for walks. Since they have a big backyard, they could also fence it in, allowing Jenny to enjoy the outdoors for more hours; she could then feel the grass, hear other animals' sounds more fully, dig holes, and otherwise engage her senses. Another possible way to enrich her life would be to get another dog. Making a point of spending more time directly interacting with Jenny would also help.

Such changes are significant, affecting a family's lifestyle and possibly entailing considerable expense – as with installing a fence. Does that mean such changes are too much to expect of human caretakers? No. The crucial point is that *keeping pets is a very serious responsibility*. As with having children, people should plan carefully and realistically before taking on pets, and should do so only if the pets' basic needs can be met – assuming the comparable-life condition is also satisfied. After all, animals have moral status and do not exist merely for human pleasure.

While the appropriateness of keeping pets depends on the details of

8. A baby gibbon on sale.

particular cases, which determine whether the two conditions are met, we may venture one sweeping generalization: it is wrong to keep exotic or undomesticated animals – such as monkeys, mice, canaries, snakes, and iguanas – as pets. It is simply unrealistic to expect to be able to care adequately for animals who are forced into living situations radically different from those for which they are naturally suited. Owners are nearly always ignorant of exotic animals' particular needs; nor can one expect veterinarians to respond adequately to their health problems. If an exotic animal does not die quickly – most do within a few years – the owner may tire of having her yet be unable to find another willing owner. Perhaps worst of all, buying undomesticated animals encourages people to capture them from the wild, thereby destroying animal families and introducing the predictable harms incurred in transport, handling, and life as a sales item.

By contrast with exotic animals, truly domesticated species such as cats and dogs present some clear genetic divergence from their ancestral wild counterparts, as in the case of dogs and wolves. Through human breeding, domesticated animals have become better suited than wild animals to live with humans. But how should one obtain a domesticated animal? There is presently a very serious problem of overpopulation with these species, resulting in both the miseries of homelessness – whether on the street, in shelters, or (in some countries) in research laboratories – and the 'euthanizing' of millions of unwanted animals each year. Since buying a pet from a store or animal breeder encourages the perpetuation of this problem, along with the neglect of animals in stores, it is far more responsible to adopt a pet from a shelter. For the same reason, it is equally important to spay or neuter a pet if he or she has not already undergone this procedure. Local governments can help by establishing low-cost sterilization clinics.

Description of zoos

Humans have kept collections of animals for many years, dating back at least to ancient Egypt. Zoological parks or zoos – parks exhibiting animals, chiefly for entertainment, educational, or scientific purposes – began to emerge in continental Europe in the eighteenth century. The first British and American zoos appeared in the nineteenth century.

Zoos would not exist if humans never took animals from the wild. The process of keeping animals in zoos begins with humans capturing wild animals and introducing them to captive life. Often, another step is that of dealing in wild animals, which frequently involves considerable neglect and cruelty. Many animals die in this process – either from an arduous journey (which may include abuse), lethal infections, or unsuccessful adjustments to the zoo environment. Human captors break up families and other social units. Additionally, the captors may slaughter family members of captured animals to facilitate capture; not long ago, for instance, chimpanzee mothers were routinely killed as their infants were apprehended.

Once animals from a particular species are captive, an alternative to further capture is to breed animals from those already in zoos. Increasingly, breeding animals of endangered species is among a zoo's stated objectives. Optimally, breeding programmes maintain genetic diversity and thereby avoid health problems stemming from inbreeding, avoid producing more animals than can be properly cared for, and release some animals to the wild. Some zoos, however, breed in order to sell surplus animals to the entertainment industry, or breed by accident when fertile animals share cages.

Zoos vary enormously in quality. The range includes 'zoos' that are not really zoological parks; the most desolate of these are roadside menageries featuring one or more isolated, caged animals. Some larger menageries house animals in small, barren cages that in no way encourage visitors to respect wildlife; nor do they educate, facilitate research, or help with species preservation. But even true zoological parks vary greatly. Some are about as bleak as the menageries just described. Others, like the National Zoo in Washington, DC, feature both good exhibits and poor ones. The best tend to have fewer species, provide a great deal of space, and sometimes almost reproduce the animals' natural habitats – minus most of the dangers. My admittedly only literature-based impression is that some of the finest zoos are Zoo Atlanta, the Bronx Zoo-Wildlife Conservation Park, San Diego Wild Animal Park, and Scotland's Edinburgh Zoo and Glasgow Zoo. Partly in response to criticisms from animal advocates, the current trend among 'the cream of the crop' is away from cages towards naturalistic habitats, making zoos less like prisons and more like bioparks.

Should we take animals from the wild?

No ethical evaluation of zoos can avoid the question of animal procurement. Should humans continue to take animals from the wild? In addressing this question, we must consider the associated harms. In view of what we know about the mental lives of vertebrate animals – as most zoo animals are vertebrates – we may assume that capture commonly imposes pain, fear, anxiety, and suffering on animals. In the case of social animals, breaking up families or other social groups is likely to cause sadness or other forms of distress; and, again, some group members may be killed to facilitate capture. Transporting captive animals entails confining them in our sense – they do not live well while cooped up – and may result in injury or death. Introducing stressed creatures into an alien environment presumably causes unpleasant experiences and frequently leads to health problems and sometimes death shortly after arrival. All told, this process predictably causes unpleasant feelings and temporary confinement and often results in death; sometimes disease and injury are part of the picture. *In view of these harms, there is a very strong moral presumption against taking animals from the wild*. Can any of the major purposes of zoos justify overriding this presumption in particular cases? Might the harms in question count as necessary?

Of the four major purposes of zoos, three of them – entertainment, scientific research, and education – are largely human-centred. Entertainment is purely for our sake and is not weighty enough to justify inflicting significant suffering and other harms; it would be weighty enough only if animals lacked moral status and were mere objects for our use. While animal research primarily serves human interests, it sometimes benefits animals by improving our ability to care for them. Then again, most research does not depend on zoos. Meanwhile, education is at least primarily for our sake. But, recently, some zoo advocates have argued that zoos can and should educate visitors about the importance of conservation and species preservation, ultimately benefiting animals by changing attitudes and inspiring activism. The likelihood that such benefits will actually reach animals, however, is uncertain. It is also unclear why, in our multimedia world, this sort of education requires zoos. In any case, even if some animal-benefiting research or education truly requires zoos, there are already many animals in captivity. The alternative of planned breeding casts major

9. An orang-utan walking on ropes.

doubt on the supposed necessity of capturing more animals from the wild.

Can the goal of species preservation justify further capture from the wild? Today many zoos portray themselves as promoting the survival of endangered species. Indeed, some zoo advocates identify species preservation as *the* major goal of zoos – although small portions of zoo budgets are devoted to this endeavour. One advantage of this goal is that nearly everyone endorses it. Yet its importance is disputable. If a species goes out of existence, there is no meaningful sense in which the *species* is harmed; species are not beings with interests and so cannot be harmed. (Indeed, species are groupings determined as much by human convention as by biological reality.) To be sure, changes in an ecosystem, including those resulting from extinction, affect individual animals. But the difference to an ecosystem between the extinction of species X and a few members of X surviving is negligible – especially if they survive only in zoos! As Jamieson notes, species preservation is primarily a *human desire*. While species preservation may be desirable in the absence of conflicts, its importance becomes very questionable when it conflicts with the welfare of particular animals – for example, when animals are seriously harmed in the process of capture, transport, and introduction to zoos. The captured animals themselves do not benefit from species preservation. Indeed, it is unclear that any animals do, given the reality of zoos' efforts at species preservation.

Zoos have, in fact, made serious efforts to protect only a small number of species, and have successfully reintroduced just a few to the wild; so far most reintroduction efforts have failed. Moreover, breeding sometimes produces surplus animals who are auctioned off or even 'euthanized'. Breeding with a small number of individuals often leads to inbreeding, producing young animals with increased vulnerability to disease and environmental stresses. While at least a few zoos are doing good species-preservation work, this usually takes place at remote breeding facilities where visitors are unwelcome. This casts further doubt on the need for zoos – and especially for the capture of more wild animals – for species preservation. Meanwhile, there is an alternative means to this goal that is much more likely to be effective: *curtailing human devastation of the environment*.

For all of these reasons, humans should stop capturing wild animals for zoo exhibits. Are there exceptions? Fred Koontz, a zoo advocate, argues that capture is sometimes necessary to increase genetic diversity among captive animals of endangered species, thereby decreasing the risk of inbreeding. The plausibility of this argument turns mainly on the importance of species preservation and the viability of pursuing this goal through zoos; reasonable doubts on either score weaken the argument. In principle, a stronger justification for the capture of particular wild animals is that *they themselves* would benefit. One might claim this of certain animals whose environment, which there is no way to improve, poses great danger. But, for the animals to benefit on balance, zoo life must be so much better than life in the wild that the benefits of zoo life offset the various harms incurred in capture, transport, and introduction to the zoo. Even if this is sometimes the case, it is hard to be optimistic about trusting zoo representatives – who are responsive to many interests, including self-serving ones – to make such judgements impartially. If any exceptions to the 'no more wild capture' rule are really worth granting, they are more likely to involve 'lower' species, in which less rich mental lives may entail less harm in the transition from the wild to captivity.

Should we keep animals in zoos?

Regarding already captive animals, is it right to keep them in zoos at all? Consider our two lions, Leo and Leona, from the beginning of this chapter. Although they are well fed, disease-free, and comfortable, their living situation is devoid of enrichment and of the company of lions other than each other. They are bored, get little exercise, and never fully engage their physical and mental capacities. Whether they would likely be better off in the wild, where enrichment would be accompanied by many dangers, is disputable. But even if the comparable-life condition is met, the basic-needs condition is not, due to the neglect of the lions' needs for companionship, exercise, and stimulation. Keeping Leo and Leona in these conditions is therefore unjustified.

Together, the two conditions for keeping animals establish tough standards that probably only a small fraction of current zoo exhibits satisfy. Yet, in the case of most species, these standards *are* achievable with sufficient imagination, space, and expenditure. Most animals' basic needs can be met in captivity if conditions are sufficiently favourable. As for determining whether captive life can be as good as life in the wild, we must think realistically about the wild and avoid temptations to romanticize it. (Although the most severe critics of zoos may be right on most counts, they commonly make two errors: (1) thinking all captivity is harmful or disrespectful and (2) overlooking the disadvantages of life in the wild.) Wild animals regularly face the risks of disease and injuries, harsh weather, food shortages, and predators. Well-managed zoos offer consistent nourishment, protection from harsh weather and predators, and veterinary care. In zoos, animals may be able to live longer – which must generally count as a benefit, since death is a harm (see Chapter 4) – and avoid many sources of suffering.

What would enable zoos to meet the two conditions for keeping animals? Besides the obvious imperatives of adequate food, available shelter, and veterinary care, key features include ample space for exercise, preservation of species-typical social groups (for social species), and creative enrichment of living spaces – preferably in something resembling their natural habitats. Creative sources of enrichment can make animals' lives more stimulating, invigorating, and healthful. Ways to provide enrichment include hiding food, placing it in boxes or other unusual containers, or putting it where animals must climb or jump to obtain it, assuming the inconvenience is not cruel; arranging more feedings of smaller amounts rather than one or two large daily feedings; and providing a variety of objects to explore, manipulate, and hide behind. At the National Zoo in Washington, DC, orang utans have the opportunity to participate in rudimentary language training, a novel form of enrichment. No doubt the most enriched and otherwise excellent exhibits are those that blur the boundary between zoos and bioparks, offering animals a rough approximation of their natural environs, minus most of the dangers.

Probably a few zoos already meet the basic-needs and comparable-life conditions. Some other zoos might be able to improve enough to meet them. *Those that cannot or will not improve sufficiently to meet these conditions should close.* In the case of 'lower' vertebrates, who may have less capacity for suffering and whose loss from confinement may be smaller, one might argue that the goals of education, research, and species preservation sometimes justify exceptions to these conditions. On the other hand, the simpler needs of these animals make it easier to

10. A rhinoceros.

satisfy the two conditions – and an invitation to make exceptions seems dangerously open to self-serving abuse. There is a good case, then, against allowing exceptions. (Those who reject equal consideration in favour of the sliding-scale model may embrace only the basic-needs condition and, on that basis, regard more zoos and zoo exhibits as passing moral muster.)

Because, for most people, visiting zoos is an occasional activity that costs little, boycotting unacceptable zoos would be ineffective. Probably legislation is necessary to ensure compliance with standards like our two conditions. Menageries cannot meet such standards and should be banned. It would also probably be wisest to prohibit private zoos more generally. Given the depressing history of zoos, and the tendency of zoo advocates to cloak self-serving or at least human-serving interests in the guise of animal-welfare rhetoric, the profit motive seems too likely to underwrite neglect and mistreatment of zoo animals. In the end, probably the only justified zoos will be a small number of the very finest public ones. These will probably have such large and naturalistic exhibits that animals are often hard to see. Perhaps one sign of a justified zoo will be its policy of routinely lending binoculars to visitors.

Because animals have moral status, and are not simply objects for human use, the discussion of zoos has focused on animals' interests. But the moral status of animals, I suggest, also generates a responsibility that may not be fully explicable in terms of animals' interests. That is *the responsibility to cultivate an attitude of respect for animals – as beings with moral status*. This is not respect for autonomy, a concept out of place here; nor is it a notion of respect that precludes any keeping of animals, a notion that seems groundless. It is simply a proper recognition that animals have importance in their own right and not merely as tools for human use or playthings for our entertainment. Unfortunately, zoos frequently encourage people to think animals exist *for us*, by displaying them, for our amusement, in conditions that give them sorry lives, by

95

denying them places from which they can hide from intrusive crowds, and by failing to implement positive educational measures to cultivate respect and admiration for animals. In the end, the best way to cultivate appropriate attitudes may be by simulating animals' natural habitats.

Some special cases

While the basic-needs and comparable-life conditions apply to all prospective zoo animals, a few special cases deserve mention. First, *in effect* these conditions apply only to creatures with interests, sentient animals. Animals lacking interests cannot be harmed (at least in any morally relevant sense) and therefore cannot be harmed wrongfully. They have no needs and cannot have a good or bad life. So there is no coherent case against keeping non-sentient animals or against keeping them in particular conditions – except that zoos should not exhibit them in ways that promote disrespect for animals (say, through gratuitous destruction of living beings). The case of non-sentient animals provides another reason to reject a liberation ethic that opposes all keeping of animals.

On the other end of the scale of non-human life are Great Apes and dolphins. Their cognitive, emotional, and social complexity sets a very strong presumption against keeping them in zoos or aquatic exhibits. Yet our interest in species preservation is most intense in regard to our nearest cousins, the Great Apes. Any keeping of these creatures should comply with the two conditions. That may require family preservation, a great deal of space, and considerable enrichment that encourages playing, climbing, exploring, and problem-solving. On the other hand, it is likely impossible to keep dolphins in aquatic exhibits while meeting the comparable-life condition. Their marine habit, their propensity to swim enormous distances, and their rich social organization constitute a form of life requiring an environment that we land animals probably cannot simulate. One might also doubt that captivity is compatible with meeting their basic needs. Unfortunately, we continue to take dolphins from the wild, away from their families, only to keep them in aquatic exhibits for our entertainment. The case for banning dolphin exhibits is extremely powerful.

Chapter 7
Animal research

For seventeen years, beginning in 1960, scientists at the American Museum of Natural History in New York City conducted cat sex experiments. In these experiments, the researchers mutilated cats in various ways – such as removing parts of their brains, destroying their sense of smell, and deadening their sense of touch by severing nerves in their sex organs – and then evaluated their sexual performance in different settings. Thus, for example, researchers calculated average frequencies of 'mounts' for cats deprived of their sense of smell. Although funded by the (US) National Institute of Child Health and Human Development, National Institutes of Health (NIH), how this work might have benefited children, or any human beings, was difficult to fathom. Then again, the museum's director, Thomas Nicholson, apparently did not feel any such promise of benefit was required: 'If anything has distinguished this museum, it has been its freedom to study whatever it chooses, without regard to its demonstrable practical value. . . . We intend to maintain this freedom' (quoted by Burns). While many scientists may have felt similarly in the days of this controversy, they apparently did not find this work significant even from a purely scientific standpoint; of the twenty-one articles published on the basis of the cat sex experiments, few were ever cited in the scientific literature. Nor did the public care for Nicholson's *laissez-faire* attitude about animal research, once they learnt about the experiments through the efforts of activist Henry Spira (as described, along with the experiments themselves, in Singer's book on Spira). Citizens wrote in protest to the museum, NIH, and Congress, provoking Congress to pressure NIH, which finally in 1977 stopped funding the experiments.

From the 1950s to the 1970s, Harry Harlow, a highly respected psychologist who worked at the Primate Research Center (Madison, Wisconsin), conducted experiments in which infant monkeys were raised from birth in total isolation, having contact with neither monkeys nor humans. Exploring a variety of topics – such as the factors contributing to mother–infant bonding – Harlow and colleagues studied the psychological effects of social isolation (including maternal deprivation), rejection, and various forms of torment. In most of these experiments, the infants encountered mother surrogates – some made of wire, others of cloth; some easily accessible, others untouchable due to Plexiglas boxes. The infants' behaviour *vis-à-vis* surrogates was examined in various frightening situations, which often produced such abnormal behaviours as self-clasping, rocking, and convulsive jerking. For some of these experiments, Harlow devised 'monsters' to which the mother-deprived monkeys would attempt to attach themselves. These included a cloth monkey 'mother' that ejected high-pressure compressed air, a 'mother' that rocked so violently the baby's head would rattle, one that ejected the infant with a spring, and another that suddenly emitted sharp spikes. Typically, baby monkeys kept trying to approach these monster mothers even after rejection. Later, Harlow reared female monkeys in isolation, impregnated them artificially, and kept them with their subsequently born infants; while some mothers simply ignored the infants, others attacked and in some cases killed them. Further experiments included such innovations as a 'tunnel of terror' and a 'well of despair'. (The latter experiment yielded this result: '[A] 45-day period of vertical chamber confinement early in life produced severe and persistent psychopathological behavior of a depressive nature in the experimental subjects.') While Harlow studied important

11. A caged monkey with an electrode implant.

topics, and may have illuminated aspects of mother–infant bonding, several psychologists have questioned whether he discovered anything significant that could not have been learnt without using monkeys. One might contend that this research (which is helpfully described in Singer's *Animal Liberation*; see also Orlans, Beauchamp *et al.* and Taylor) at least informed us about the effects of maternal deprivation – surely an important matter. Yet prior to Harlow's experiments, John Bowlby, a leading researcher in this area, had concluded that prolonged deprivation of maternal care had profoundly negative effects on young children. Rather than using monkeys to learn about human children, Bowlby had studied refugees, war orphans, and institutionalized children.

The cat sex experiments and Harlow's research challenge the proposition that animal research should never be constrained by concerns about animal welfare. By contrast, many experiments conducted today – for example, in the areas of AIDS and cancer – attempt to illuminate matters of vital importance to human health while limiting harms to animal subjects. To put matters in perspective, while animal research has received much more public attention and criticism than has factory farming, the moral case for animal research is stronger. For one thing, at least in many developed countries, there are now laws and regulations whose purpose is to minimize the pain and distress of research animals; protections for factory farm animals are much weaker or absent. Moreover, while estimates of the number of animals used worldwide in research range from 41 to 100 million annually, the number of animals killed in factory farms each year is over 5 billion in the USA alone. Further, one can reasonably claim that animal research, unlike factory farming, offers some highly significant, otherwise unattainable benefits. Still, it is debatable whether – and, if so, under what conditions – animal research is justified. This issue provokes fundamental questions about animals' moral status, and the differences between the three senses of 'animal rights' (see Chapter 2) prove significant in this context.

Some background

In this discussion, the term 'animal research' will be used broadly to include several different endeavours. One is *the pursuit of original scientific knowledge*. (When 'animal research' is used narrowly, it designates this endeavour and contrasts with testing and education.) This type of research divides into two subtypes: studies seeking new knowledge of biological processes and functions (basic research) and studies seeking new medical, veterinary, or biological knowledge in order to promote the health of humans, animals, or the environment (applied research). Another kind of research, *testing*, evaluates chemicals and other products for safety. Finally, animals may be used for *educational purposes*, for example, in science fair projects, dissection, and surgery practice. Since such educational uses of animals include many that are not experiments, the meaning of 'research' stretches somewhat in covering these uses.

Animal research emerged as a significant scientific activity in the early nineteenth century. Partly in response to the pioneering work of François Magendie and Claude Bernard of France, the anti-vivisection movement was born in nineteenth-century England. Despite a long history, organized opposition to animal research did not halt a single experiment until NIH pulled the plug on the cat sex experiments in 1977. By that time, there were some laws and regulations applying to animal research.

In the United States, widespread outrage followed the revelation in 1966 that pet dogs were being stolen, abused by animal dealers, and sold to research laboratories. That same year the Laboratory Animal Welfare Act, which was primarily a pet-protection bill, became law. Subsequent amendments – which shortened the name to 'Animal Welfare Act' – increased requirements for the care and use of research animals. Their provisions addressed the use of pain-relieving drugs, size requirements for cages, and the establishment of Institutional Animal Care and Use Committees within a system in which institutions receiving federal funds largely policed themselves.

While American legislation clearly represents progress in the protection of animals, it is often criticized by animal advocates and by representatives of Western Europe, where protections for animals tend to be somewhat stronger. For one thing, the Animal Welfare Act does not cover farm animals, birds, reptiles, amphibians, or fish. Incredibly, it does not even cover the most commonly used research subjects: rats and mice. The situation could change, however, in October 2001. A new US Department of Agriculture rule expanding regulation to cover birds, rats, and mice will go into effect unless congressional meddling blocks the rule for a second consecutive year. In any case, Public Health Service policy covers all vertebrate animals in PHS-funded research. Another reason for concern is that one of the published principles that are supposed to guide the care and use of animals begins with implicit permission to make exceptions to all the others: 'Where exceptions are required in relation to the provision of these Principles, . . . ' The principles state no limits on permissible exceptions. By contrast, the *International Guiding Principles for Biomedical Research Involving Animals* avoids the pitfall of such a global loophole.

In Great Britain the early anti-vivisection movement (see Chapter 1) touched enough of the public to ensure passage of the Cruelty to Animals Act in 1876, which protected research animals in particular. According to Robert Garner's historical analysis, this Act had an impact on the conduct of animal researchers, preventing major abuses and probably discouraging some animal experiments that would otherwise have been carried out. A Royal Commission appointed in 1906 effected several reforms, including the appointment of full-time inspectors and a rule requiring the painless killing of animals who suffered severe, enduring pain. Concern about research animals flared up again in the 1960s and 1970s, as the contemporary animal rights movement got under way, but the British public had to wait until 1986 for the next major legal reform, the Animals (Scientific Procedures) Act. As Garner explains, the new Act required researchers to obtain a personal licence – to be reviewed every five years – and a project licence for particular experimental procedures. Additionally, it created an Animal Procedures Committee, whose representatives would include animal advocates, and required animal breeders and suppliers to register and submit to inspections.

Throughout the history of animal research, and throughout the world, proponents have consistently claimed important benefits on its behalf. Noting that animal studies have played a role in the development of myriad new medical therapies and techniques – and in the advancement of basic biological knowledge – proponents cite progress in the areas of Alzheimer's disease, AIDS, basic genetics, cancer, cardiovascular disease, haemophilia, malaria, organ transplantation, treatment of spinal cord injuries, and countless others. While the vast bulk of animal research is intended to advance human interests, proponents remind us that additional benefits involve our ability to care for animals. Examples include superior medicines and techniques for treating sick or injured pets, antibiotics to treat bovine mastitis, and, through behavioural research, improved conservation of wild animals.

Difficulties in assessing the value of animal research

In the case of many biomedical advances, animal research has indisputably been part of the pathway to progress. *But it does not follow that animal research was necessary for such progress.* Analogously, just because you gave me a ride to the subway doesn't mean I needed the ride to get there; perhaps I could have walked or taken a bus. Indeed, some critics would claim that we have made biomedical progress *despite* animal research.

These critics doubt that non-human animals are good scientific models for human beings. Obviously, mice, dogs, and monkeys are not humans. And it is probably fair to say that animal models *can* be misleading, with serious consequences. Hugh LaFollette and Niall Shanks contend, for example, that reliance on misleading animal models delayed the development of an effective polio vaccine for many years.

Still, it is reasonable to assume that, due to biological and psychological similarities across species, well-chosen animal models often provide valuable information on the road to biomedical advances. But what if there are other, non-animal roads to progress? The case for animal research is much weaker if animal use is unnecessary. Hence the crucial question: how great are the benefits that *only* animal research can deliver?

This is an extremely complex issue. Addressing it requires comparing (1) the progress that results, or has resulted, from actual use of animal subjects against (2) the progress that could result, or could have resulted, from the best possible non-animal models. Estimating (2) requires speculation because it is hypothetical. Unless animal research advocates can make this comparison pretty convincingly – as I doubt they can – then while they may correctly claim that animal research has yielded benefits, they are in no position to claim that animal research was *necessary* for those benefits. Furthermore, we must remember that in animal research particular benefits are only *possible and hoped for*, whereas the harms to animal subjects are immediate and certain. (Thus, countless experiments harm animals without yielding benefits.) Any honest cost–benefit analysis must multiply the value of some hoped-for benefit *against the likelihood of achieving it*, before weighing that estimate against the predictable harms. In light of (1) the issue of non-animal alternatives and (2) the need to factor in likelihood of success to generate an honest cost–benefit analysis, the value of animal research would seem to be less than proponents typically assert.

Do important ends justify harmful means?

Let us assume some animal research promises otherwise unattainable benefits. Does that justify using animal subjects – who, obviously, cannot give informed consent – in ways that harm them? It is commonly thought that a favourable benefit–cost ratio, where the benefits are otherwise unattainable, would automatically justify a particular use of animals. But that doesn't follow. After all, the mere fact that using human subjects in a particular way would offer otherwise unattainable benefits and a favourable benefit–cost ratio does not automatically justify an experiment. We recognize ethical limits to the use of humans – as reflected, for example, in requirements for the informed consent of competent adult subjects and for risks to be reasonable in relation to expected benefits. These ethical limits serve as side-constraints within which biomedical researchers must work. Thus, we have long accepted that we must forgo some potentially valuable studies, such as promising pediatric research in which subjects face great risks without standing to benefit.

Therefore, the key issue with animals is whether their moral status precludes or limits their use in research regardless of potential benefits. A strong animal-rights view – which understands rights in the utility-trumping sense – rejects the harming of some individuals (without their consent) for others' benefit. This position almost precludes the use of animals in research, but not quite. It allows (1) research that does not harm its animal subjects at all and (2) therapeutic veterinary research – that is, research that is in the best interests of the animal subjects themselves (say, where there is no established method for treating their ailment).

A strong animal-rights view *might* accept one further category of animal research. At first glance, it appears that equal consideration would support non-therapeutic animal research posing *only minimal risk* to subjects. For nearly everyone accepts the minimal-risk standard for human children – who, like animals, cannot give informed consent. But while strong animal-rights advocates accept equal consideration, it is possible that they would reject the imposition of even very small known risks on animals – or human children – in non-therapeutic research. They might argue that the minimal-risk standard does not adequately respect children's rights to protection.

Whether or not a strong animal-rights view would accept the minimal-risk standard for animals, another equal-consideration theory, utilitarianism, clearly does. In fact, utilitarians go further. They accept animal research posing more-than-minimal risk so long as the promised benefits – factoring in the likelihood of achieving them and giving animals' interests equal weight to humans' comparable interests – outweigh the costs, and no alternative offers a better benefit–cost ratio. Now utilitarians who apply their theory correctly (unlike 'utilitarians' who give animals' interests diminished weight across the board) typically assert that very little animal research is justified. Still, because they allow some non-therapeutic research that falls into the present category of more-than-minimal risk, utilitarians such as Peter Singer arrive at a position that is notably different from that of strong animal-rights theorists such as Tom Regan. Note that utilitarianism is also, at least in principle, open to the involuntary use of *humans* in research.

Compared with utilitarianism, the sliding-scale approach – which, for example, grants animal suffering less moral weight than human suffering – would be considerably more welcoming of animal research. Then again, because it attributes moral status to animals, denying that they are mere tools for our use, this approach would probably reject a great deal of current animal research, especially where it involves 'higher' animals. Examples include experiments lacking real benefits (for example, the cat sex experiments), research offering non-essential benefits (for example, testing of new cosmetics), research causing excessive harm (for example, many or all of Harlow's studies), and uses of animals that are clearly replaceable (for example, many educational uses).

Harms and costs

Having explored the possible benefits of animal research, and the issue of whether and to what extent such benefits justify harming animal subjects, we must now consider the relevant harms as well as other associated costs. Beginning with harms caused in experimental procedures, they range from none to extreme. Merely observing animals in field studies does not harm them. Taking a simple blood sample or vaginal smear sample from a laboratory animal will probably involve only minimal discomfort. Taking frequent blood samples, on the other hand, or holding an animal in restraints – say, in an inhalation chamber – might count as a moderate harm; similarly with performing a caesarian section on a pregnant animal. Examples of severe harms include prolonged deprivation of sleep, food, or water; the induction of cancer tumours; the causing of brain damage (as in a well-known University of Pennsylvania head-trauma study using baboons); and force-feeding animals a substance until half of them die (as in LD50 tests of new products).

Typically, animal subjects are killed, either during an experiment or afterwards. Although it is most plausible to hold that death harms animals as well as humans (whether or not to the same degree – see Chapter 4), current animal research policies suggest otherwise by including provisions for the minimization of pain and distress but none for the avoidance of killing. This oversimplified view of animals' interests implies that an experiment that imposes no experiential harm to animals but ends with their 'sacrifice' is harmless. While a death that terminates otherwise unavoidable suffering may constitute the lesser of possible evils, death is a form of harm that we must not ignore.

Harms caused to animal subjects can also include conditions of housing. Research animals frequently live in small cages featuring highly unnatural living conditions with little or no enrichment. Boredom and lack of companionship are common. While current American regulations require exercise for dogs and psychological enrichment for primates, the vast majority of research subjects are 'lower' mammals who are not protected by such requirements. In Chapter 6, two standards for keeping animals were defended: animals' basic physical and psychological needs must be met, and animals must be provided with a life that is at least as good as they would likely have in the wild. Currently, housing conditions for research animals seldom meet these two conditions. With sufficient expenditure, imagination, and dedication, researchers can probably meet these conditions in the case of nearly all species. Researchers can even solicit the input of animals themselves by giving them a choice of living conditions and observing which they select (one of several useful suggestions made by Smith and Boyd). Housing that meets the above two conditions is not only ethically sound; it would also promote good science, because stress, disease, and other unnecessary harms can introduce inconsistencies among animal subjects, confounding data.

The handling of animal subjects can also introduce harm. Rough handling, such as forcibly subduing an animal before giving her an injection, can cause extreme distress and pain; later, memory of the traumatic encounter can cause fear when the handler returns. By contrast, gentle handling that includes positive reinforcement for the animal's co-operation can largely avoid such harms, especially if supplemented by rapport-building handling and grooming that takes place independently of experimental procedures.

The acquisition of research animals is yet another possible source of harm. Where animals are transported from some location outside the laboratory, that process can range from benign to very stressful. What is the proper source of animal subjects? The American biomedical research community has long lobbied for its 'right' to use dogs and cats taken from shelters or pounds – thereby lowering costs – and to acquire animals from the wild. This position is dubious, however. As we saw in discussing zoos (Chapter 6), taking animals from the wild involves so many harms that it should rarely, if ever, occur. Meanwhile, the transformation of former pets into laboratory subjects is likely to be very stressful and frightening for them. Acquiring animals this way also indirectly encourages the pet homelessness problem, by putting overpopulation to 'good use', and arguably perverts the idea of shelters as animal sanctuaries. Far preferable, I suggest, is the alternative of using animals bred specifically for research – as the laws of Britain and numerous other European countries require.

In addition to the harms we have discussed, one further cost merits careful consideration: money. Government-funded research uses taxpayers' money. Where for-profit companies fund research – say, in product testing – stockholders' money is used. Obviously, while alternatives that do not use animals do not harm them, such alternatives do entail financial costs.

Having sketched the major harms and costs of animal research, let us

Three standards for using animals in research

Strong animal-rights view

Animals may be used in research only where (1) their involvement does not harm them or (2) their involvement is in their overall best interests (therapeutic research). This view might also permit animals to be used in research where (3) their involvement poses only minimal risk to them.

Utilitarianism

Animals may be used in research only where their use is likely to maximize the overall balance of benefits – factoring in likelihood of success – over harms, where all parties' (including animals') interests are impartially considered.

Sliding-scale model

Animals may be used in research only where their use is consistent with giving their interests appropriate moral weight in view of the animals' cognitive, emotional, and social complexity.

confront a frequently raised question: is there a degree of harm that animal subjects should never undergo, regardless of potential benefits? On the other side of cost–benefit considerations, how promising must a proposed experiment be to be justified?

We may address both questions from the viewpoints we have been examining. On a strong animal-rights view, no involvement of animals in non-therapeutic research should harm them – or, at any rate, subject them to more-than-minimal risk. Since *all* harms to animal subjects count, housing conditions must meet the basic-needs and comparable-life standards. Meanwhile, the promise of the proposed research does not seem to enter in as a crucial factor. By contrast, utilitarianism will permit some exceptions to the minimal-risk standard and the two conditions for keeping animals if there is no less harmful way to maximize the balance of benefits over harms. How promising an experiment must be can only be determined holistically, in conjunction with considering harms and costs; there is, in principle, neither a maximum permissible harm nor a minimum required promise of benefit. But, since utilitarianism counts equally animal and human suffering, and since research benefits are only hoped for, this theory will probably support only research that addresses pressing medical needs and will very rarely permit great harm to animal subjects. Like utilitarianism, the sliding-scale view offers no formulas regarding permissible harm to subjects or required promise of benefits. In light of the harms and expense typically associated with animal research, however, it would seem that proposed studies would have to be rather compelling, on this view, to justify those costs.

Alternatives

In our earlier discussion of whether important benefits justify harming animals, we assumed that there were no viable alternatives to animal use in seeking those benefits. Let us now confront the issue of alternatives. Since viable alternatives would eliminate or reduce the harms associated with research, they should be pursued very vigorously.

But what, exactly, are alternatives? Sometimes the term refers only to the *replacement* of whole-animal use with other methods, especially *in vitro* – literally, *in glass* – studies. But often the term refers more broadly to 'the three R's' (as introduced by Russell and Burch): in addition to replacement, *reduction* of the number of animals required for an experiment and *refinement* of existing techniques so as to minimize animals' pain, distress, and suffering. Reductions are sometimes accomplished by superior statistical techniques that lower the number of animal subjects necessary to achieve significant results. Examples of refinements include the following: acclimatizing animals to the experimental situation before performing a procedure, reducing stress; optimal use of anaesthesia and analgesia to reduce pain; good handling techniques; enrichment of animals' living conditions, which reduces boredom and promotes health; and humane endpoints such as specific clinical indicators, rather than death, as an endpoint in toxicity tests or vaccine potency tests. The Humane Society of the United States' initiative to find ways to eliminate all significant pain and distress in laboratory animals by 2020 focuses on refinements.

In addition to promoting animal welfare, alternatives are sometimes preferable on scientific or economic grounds. In some cases non-animal methods are the most straightforward means of answering particular questions – a major reason for the trend toward use of *in vitro* methods in pharmacology, biochemistry, and related fields. Often it is possible to utilize human organs, tissues, or cells, or even human volunteers, making it unnecessary to extrapolate from animal data to the human situation. And sometimes non-animal methods are less costly than animal use.

Although strongly endorsed by animal protection organizations and popular with the general public, the alternatives movement still encounters resistance from within the biomedical research community and faces other obstacles. After the Second World War, new regulations requiring animal studies before human studies, generous funding for biomedicine, and the explosive development of the chemical industry helped to fuel a strong tradition of beginning biomedical research with animal studies. Tradition, of course, breeds habits, and habits – such as thinking in terms of animal models – die slowly. Moreover, some leaders in biomedicine who feared animal rights activists felt that accepting alternatives would convey to the public that they were 'giving in' to activists. Additionally, even today there is insufficient recognition of the three R's as a well-developed scientific discipline. Compounding these difficulties is the virtual absence of public funding for the development of alternatives – although some parties within the private sector have been quite generous. Despite these difficulties, recent years have witnessed much progress in developing alternatives in education, testing, and original research.

Medical and veterinary schools have long used live animals for physiology and pharmacology demonstrations as well as for surgery practice. Animal use has also been common for dissection in high school classes and in student exhibits at high school science fairs. Alternatives have begun to make inroads, however. For example, medical, veterinary, and high school students now often use interactive computer models or other audiovisual guides for certain educational purposes, gaining the advantage of repeated viewing – of both animal and human models. Meanwhile, heightened public concern about animal welfare has evidently led participants in American science fairs to exercise greater restraint – in the form of either reduced numbers or refined techniques – in using animals. Such restraint is independent of legal sanctions, though, because the Animal Welfare Act exempts elementary and secondary schools from its requirements. By contrast, Britain prohibits students below the undergraduate level from performing interventions likely to cause pain or suffering to vertebrate animals, while many European nations have laws restricting animal use in elementary and secondary schools.

New products such as pesticides, drugs, shampoos, and cosmetics are routinely tested on live animals for safety before they reach the market. In the USA, a great deal of testing is not subject to government regulations on animal use because many companies receive no public funding. But two animal tests, the LD50 and Draize tests, met widespread criticism – due largely to Henry Spira's work – and inspired the alternatives movement; these tests are now used much less frequently. The LD50 test, again, force-feeds a product, such as lipstick, to animals until half of them die. In the Draize test, potentially toxic

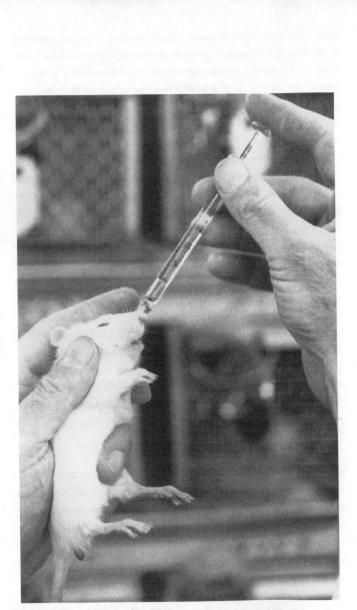

12. A mouse undergoing the LD50 test.

substances are applied directly to conscious rabbits' eyes until they are massively damaged. As a result of growing public concerns about such tests, the Johns Hopkins University Center for Alternatives to Animal Testing was established in 1981 with contributions from Avon, Bristol-Myers, and other companies with long histories of testing. Two years later the Food and Drug Administration announced that it no longer required LD50 data. Alternatives to standard toxicity tests include the Limit Test, in which a very small number of rodents receive a single dose of a test substance to see if any die (an approach combining reduction and refinement), and the use of Corrositex, a kind of synthetic skin (an example of replacement). Additionally, some new chemicals have been withdrawn from consideration after computer programmes demonstrated their toxicity. In 2000, three US federal agencies agreed to accept chemical safety data from the Corrositex test in lieu of animal tests. In the same year, the European Union accepted three *in vitro* toxicity tests into its official guidelines, meaning that where these tests are feasible the fifteen member nations will prohibit animal tests.

While alternatives have clearly made significant inroads in education and testing, and few would doubt that refinements and reductions are possible in original research, one might doubt the feasibility of replacing animals in original research. 'There's no substitute for the real thing', one hears. Yet, ultimately, the 'real thing' is the human being, since the purpose of nearly all animal research that seeks original scientific knowledge is to provide data useful to biomedicine! In any case, there have been significant advances in the development of replacement alternatives in this area, some of which involve human beings. Epidemiological studies, for example, can help to identify factors contributing to particular human diseases. In some cases human volunteers can participate, without prior animal trials, in testing diagnostic procedures or in physiological studies. Another growth area is the use of cultures of tissues and cells – both animal and human. For example, human cell tumour lines can be grown *in vitro* and then used in various studies, replacing the use of live animals. Hundreds of institutions now use human neuronal cell culture lines for basic research. Cell cultures have also, in some instances, replaced animal use in virology studies, monoclonal antibody production, and vaccine tests – although an animal may have been killed solely for the purpose of supplying cells. Sometimes computer modelling is useful in simulating biological and chemical systems. Another recent development is use of new imaging technology – such as ultrasound, magnetic resonance imaging, and PET scans – allowing study of the live human brain and body without invasive procedures on humans or animals.

How far can alternatives take us? Not so long ago many people believed, incorrectly, that non-animal methods for toxicity testing were impossible. So we must be wary of pessimistic forecasts. On the other hand, glib pronouncements that non-animal methods can replace all use of animals and maintain *the same level* of research progress seem naïve – or at least insufficiently supported by evidence. But, as noted earlier, laudable goals do not self-evidently justify harmful means. From the standpoint of those who take animals seriously, just as ethics limits the uses to which we may put humans in research – despite their being the best possible scientific model – ethics also limits the justifiable use of animals. Animals, after all, are not mere tools. Perhaps the further development of viable alternatives represents the common ground where animal advocates and biomedicine can meet.

References, sources, and further reading

Chapter 1

Bekoff, Marc (ed.), *Encyclopedia of Animal Rights and Animal Welfare* (Westport, Conn.: Greenwood, 1998).

Egonsson, Dan, *Dimensions of Dignity: The Moral Importance of Being Human* (Dordrecht: Kluwer, 1998), chapter 1: 'Introduction'.

Griffin, Donald R., *The Question of Animal Awareness* (New York: Rockefeller University Press, 1976; rev. edn., 1981).

Hearn, Kelly, 'Film Shows Egg Farm Cruelty, Say Activists', United Press International (6 June 2001): www.vny.com/cf/News/ upidetail.cfm?QID=191910

Montgomery, Lori, 'Activists Accuse Egg Farm of Cruelty', *Washington Post* (6 June 2001), B05.

Regan, Tom, and Peter Singer (eds.), *Animal Rights and Human Obligations*, 2nd edn. (Englewood Cliffs, NJ: Prentice Hall, 1989), part I: 'Animals in the History of Western Thought'.

Singer, Peter, *Animal Liberation* (New York: New York Review of Books, 1975; rev. edn., 1990).

Taylor, Angus, *Magpies, Monkeys, and Morals: What Philosophers Say about Animal Liberation* (Peterborough, Canada: Broadview, 1999), chapter 2: 'From Aristotle to Darwin'.

Chapter 2

Carruthers, Peter, *The Animals Issue: Moral Theory in Practice* (Cambridge: Cambridge University Press, 1992).

DeGrazia, David, *Taking Animals Seriously: Mental Life and Moral Status* (Cambridge: Cambridge University Press, 1996).

Frey, R. G., *Interests and Rights: The Case Against Animals* (Oxford: Clarendon Press, 1980).

Kant, Immanuel, *Lectures on Ethics*, tr. Louis Infield (New York: Harper & Row, 1963).

Markarian, Michael, 'Victory at Last: Perseverance Pays off for Pennsylvania Pigeons', *The Fund for Animals* 32/3 (Autumn 1999), 4–5.

Midgley, Mary, *Animals and Why they Matter* (Athens, GA: University of Georgia Press, 1983).

Pluhar, Evelyn B., *Beyond Prejudice: The Moral Significance of Human and Nonhuman Animals* (Durham, NC: Duke University Press, 1995).

Regan, Tom, *The Case for Animal Rights* (Berkeley, Calif.: University of California Press, 1983).

Sapontzis, S. F., *Morals, Reason, and Animals* (Philadelphia: Temple University Press, 1987).

Singer, Peter, *Animal Liberation*, 2nd edn. (New York: New York Review of Books, 1990).

Chapter 3

Bateson, Patrick, 'Assessment of Pain in Animals', *Animal Behavior*, 42 (1991), 872–89.

Bekoff, Marc, and Dale Jamieson (eds.), *Interpretation and Explanation in the Study of Animal Behavior*, 2 vols. (Boulder, Colo.: Westview, 1990).

Bolles, Robert C., and Michael S. Fanselow, 'A Perceptual Defensive Recuperative Model of Pain and Fear', *Behavioral and Brain Research*, 3 (1980), 291–323.

Carruthers, Peter, *The Animals Issue: Moral Theory in Practice* (Cambridge: Cambridge University Press, 1992).

Cassell, Eric, 'Recognizing Suffering', *Hastings Center Report*, 21/3 (1991), 24–31.

Cavalieri, Paola, and Peter Singer (eds.), *The Great Ape Project* (New York: St Martin's Press, 1993).

Cheney, Dorothy L., and Robert M. Seyfarth, *How Monkeys See the World* (Chicago: University of Chicago Press, 1990).

Dawkins, Marian Stamp, *Through our Eyes Only: The Search for Animal Consciousness* (Oxford: Freeman, 1993).

DeGrazia, David, *Taking Animals Seriously: Mental Life and Moral Status* (Cambridge: Cambridge University Press, 1996), chapters 4–7.

—— and Andrew Rowan, 'Pain, Suffering, and Anxiety in Animals and Humans', *Theoretical Medicine*, 12 (1991), 193–211.

Eisemann, C. H., W. K. Jorgensen, *et al.*, 'Do Insects Feel Pain? – A Biological View', *Experientia*, 40 (1984), 164–7.

Frey, R. G., *Interests and Rights: The Case Against Animals* (Oxford: Clarendon Press, 1980).

Gallistel, C. R. (ed.), *Animal Cognition* (Cambridge, MA: MIT Press, 1992).

Gray, Jeffrey A., *The Neuropsychology of Anxiety* (New York: Oxford University Press, 1982).

Griffin, Donald R., *Animal Minds* (Chicago: University of Chicago Press, 1992).

Harrison, Peter, 'Do Animals Feel Pain?', *Philosophy*, 66 (1991), 25–40.

Jamieson, Dale, and Marc Bekoff, 'On Aims and Methods of Cognitive Ethology', *Philosophy of Science Association*, 2 (1993), 110–24.

Kitchen, Hyram, Arthur L. Aronson, *et al.*, 'Panel Report of the Colloquium on Recognition and Alleviation of Animal Pain and Distress', *Journal of the American Veterinary Medical Association*, 191 (1987), 1186–91.

Morton, David B., and P. H. M. Griffiths, 'Guidelines on the Recognition of Pain, Distress and Discomfort in Experimental Animals and an Hypothesis for Assessment', *Veterinary Record*, 116 (1985), 431–6.

Nielsen, M., C. Braestrup, and R. F. Squires, 'Evidence for a Late Evolutionary Appearance of a Brain-Specific Benzodiazepine Receptor', *Brain Research*, 141 (1978), 342–6.

Nixon, Marion, and John B. Messenger (eds.), *The Biology of Cephalopods* (London: Academic, 1977).

Richards, J. G., and H. Mohler, 'Benzodiazepine Receptors', *Neuropharmacology*, 23 (1984), 233–42.

Rodd, Rosemary, *Biology, Ethics and Animals* (Oxford: Clarendon Press, 1990).

Rollin, Bernard A., *The Unheeded Cry: Animal Consciousness, Animal Pain, and Science* (Oxford: Oxford University Press, 1989).

Rose, Margaret, and David Adams, 'Evidence for Pain and Suffering in Other Animals', in Gill Langley (ed.), *Animal Experimentation* (New York: Chapman & Hall, 1989).

Rowan, Andrew, Franklin M. Loew, and Joan C. Weer, *The Animal Research Controversy* (North Grafton, MA: Tufts Center for Animals and Public Policy, 1994), chapter 7: 'The Question of Animal Pain/Distress'.

Sherry, David F., 'Food Storage, Memory and Marsh Tits', *Animal Behaviour*, 30 (1982), 631–63.

Smith, Jane A., and Kenneth M. Boyd, *Lives in the Balance: The Ethics of Using Animals in Biomedical Research* (New York: Oxford University Press, 1991), chapter 4: 'Pain, Stress, and Anxiety in Animals'.

Wall, Patrick D., and Ronald Melzack (eds.), *Textbook of Pain* (Edinburgh: Churchill Livingstone, 1984).

Chapter 4

DeGrazia, David, 'Equal Consideration and Unequal Moral Status', *Southern Journal of Philosophy,* 31 (1993), 17–31.

—— *Taking Animals Seriously: Mental Life and Moral Status* (Cambridge: Cambridge University Press, 1996), chapter 8: 'The Basics of Well-Being across Species'.

Frey, R. G., 'Animal Parts, Human Wholes', in James M. Humber and Robert F. Almeder (eds.), *Biomedical Ethics Reviews 1987* (Clifton, NJ: Humana, 1987), 89–107.

Rachels, James, 'Why Animals have a Right to Liberty', in Tom Regan and Peter Singer (eds.), *Animal Rights and Human Obligations*, 2nd edn. (Englewood Cliffs, NJ: Prentice Hall, 1989), 122–31.

Regan, Tom, *The Case for Animal Rights* (Berkeley, CA: University of California Press, 1983).

Rollin, Bernard E., *Animal Rights and Human Morality*, 2nd edn. (Buffalo, NY: Prometheus, 1992).

Sapontzis, S. F., *Morals, Reason, and Animals* (Philadelphia: Temple University Press, 1987).

Singer, Peter, *Practical Ethics*, 2nd edn. (Cambridge: Cambridge University Press, 1993), chapter 5: 'Taking Life: Animals'.

Chapter 5

Adcock, Melanie, 'The Truth Behind "A Hen's Life"', *HSUS News* (Spring 1993).

—— and Mary Finelli, 'The Dairy Cow: America's "Foster Mother"', *HSUS News* (Winter 1995).

Bekoff, Marc (ed.), *Encyclopedia of Animal Rights and Animal Welfare* (Westport, Conn.: Greenwood, 1988).

DeGrazia, David, *Taking Animals Seriously: Mental Life and Moral Status* (Cambridge: Cambridge University Press, 1996), chapter 9: 'Back to Animal Ethics'.

Eisnitz, Gail A., *Slaughterhouse* (Amherst, NY: Prometheus, 1997).

Fox, Michael W., 'BGH Causes National Brouhaha', *HSUS News* (Spring 1994).

Garner, Robert, *Political Animals* (London: Macmillan, 1998), chapter 7: 'The Politics of Farm Animal Welfare in Britain'.

Humane Society of the United States, 'Environmental Fact Sheet' (1994).

—— 'Fact Sheet on Broiler Chickens' (1983).

—— 'Fact Sheet on Hogs' (1983).

—— 'Human Health Fact Sheet' (1994).

—— 'Questions and Answers about Veal' (1990).

Kaufman, Marc, 'In Pig Farming, Growing Concern', *The Washington Post* (18 June 2001), A1, A7.

Lappé, Frances Moore, and Joseph Collins, *World Hunger: Twelve Myths* (New York: Grove, 1986).

Regan, Tom, *The Case for Animal Rights* (Berkeley, Calif.: University of California Press, 1983).

Singer, Peter, *Animal Liberation*, 2nd edn. (New York: New York Review of Books, 1990), chapter 3: 'Down on the Factory Farm'.

—— *Ethics into Action: Henry Spira and the Animal Rights Movement* (Lanham, MD: Rowman & Littlefield, 1998).

—— 'Utilitarianism and Vegetarianism', *Philosophy and Public Affairs*, 9 (1980), 325–37.

Warrick, Joby, 'An Outbreak Waiting to Happen', *The Washington Post* (9 Apr. 2001), A1, A10–11.

—— ' "They Die Piece by Piece" ', *The Washington Post* (10 Apr. 2001), A1, A10–11.

Chapter 6

Bekoff, Marc (ed.), *Encyclopedia of Animal Rights and Animal Welfare* (Westport, Conn.: Greenwood, 1998).

Bostock, Stephen St C., *Zoos and Animal Rights* (London: Routledge, 1993).

Cherfas, Jeremy, *Zoo 2000* (London: British Broadcasting Co., 1984).

DeGrazia, David, *Taking Animals Seriously: Mental Life and Moral Status* (Cambridge: Cambridge University Press, 1996), chapter 9: 'Back to Animal Ethics'.

Grandy, John W., 'Captive Breeding in Zoos', *HSUS News* (Summer 1989).

—— 'Zoos: A Critical Reevaluation', *HSUS News* (Summer 1992).

Hediger, H., *Wild Animals in Captivity* (New York: Dover, 1964).

Humane Society of the United States, 'Fact Sheet: Captive Wild Animal Protection Bill' (1985).

—— 'Pet Overpopulation Facts' (1999).

—— 'Zoos' (1984).

Jamieson, Dale, 'Against Zoos', in Peter Singer (ed.), *In Defense of Animals* (Oxford: Blackwell, 1985), 108–17.

—— 'Wildlife Conservation and Individual Animal Welfare', in Bryan G. Norton *et al.* (eds.), *Ethics on the Ark: Zoos, Animal Welfare, and Wildlife Conservation* (Washington, DC: Smithsonian, 1995), 69–73.

—— 'Zoos Reconsidered', in Bryan G. Norton *et al.* (eds.), *Ethics on the*

Ark: Zoos, Animal Welfare, and Wildlife Conservation (Washington, DC: Smithsonian, 1995), 52–66.

Koebner, Linda, *Zoo Book: The Evolution of Wildlife Conservation Centers* (New York: Forge, 1994).

Koontz, Fred, 'Wild Animal Acquisition Ethics for Zoo Biologists', in Bryan G. Norton *et al.* (eds.), *Ethics on the Ark: Zoos, Animal Welfare, and Wildlife Conservation* (Washington, DC: Smithsonian, 1995), 127–45.

Maple, Terry, 'Toward a Responsible Zoo Agenda', in Bryan G. Norton *et al.* (eds.), *Ethics on the Ark: Zoos, Animal Welfare, and Wildlife Conservation* (Washington, DC: Smithsonian, 1995), 20–30.

—— Rita McManamon, and Elizabeth Stevens, 'Animal Care, Maintenance, and Welfare', in Bryan G. Norton *et al.* (eds.), *Ethics on the Ark: Zoos, Animal Welfare, and Wildlife Conservation* (Washington, DC: Smithsonian, 1995), 219–34.

Regan, Tom, 'Are Zoos Morally Defensible?', in Bryan G. Norton *et al.* (eds.), *Ethics on the Ark: Zoos, Animal Welfare, and Wildlife Conservation* (Washington, DC: Smithsonian, 1995), 38–51.

Chapter 7

ALTWEB, 'First *In Vitro* Toxicity Tests Approved for Use in Europe' (altweb.jhsph.edu/altnews/archive/2000/june).

—— 'Synthetic Skin System Can Replace Animals in Some Tests of Chemical Safety' (altweb.jhsph.edu/altnews/archive/2000/march).

Bowlby, John, *Maternal Care and Mental Health* (Geneva: World Health Organization, 1952).

Burns, John F., 'American Museum Pinched for Funds', *New York Times* (16 Feb. 1976), 23.

Council for International Organizations of Medical Sciences, *International Guiding Principles for Biomedical Research Involving Animals* (Geneva: CIOMS, 1985).

Garner, Robert, *Political Animals* (London: Macmillan, 1998), chapter 9: 'The Politics of Animal Research in Britain'.

Harlow, Harry F., and Robert R. Zimmerman, 'Affectional Responses in the Infant Monkey', *Science*, 130 (1959), 421–32.

Humane Society of the United States, *HSUS Pain and Distress Initiative* (www.hsus.org/programs/research/pain_distress.html).

Johns Hopkins Center for Alternatives to Animal Testing 12/2 (Winter 1995).

LaFollette, Hugh, and Niall Shanks, *Brute Science: Dilemmas of Animal Experimentation* (London: Routledge, 1996), chapter 8: 'Causal Disanalogy II: The Empirical Evidence'.

National Research Council, *Guide for the Care and Use of Laboratory Animals* (Washington, DC: National Academy Press, 1996), appendix D: 'Public Health Service Policy and Government Principles Regarding the Care and Use of Animals'.

Orlans, F. Barbara, *In the Name of Science: Issues in Responsible Animal Experimentation* (New York: Oxford University Press, 1993).

Orlans, F. Barbara, Tom Beauchamp *et al., The Human Use of Animals: Case Studies in Ethical Choice* (New York: Oxford University Press, 1998), chapter 9: 'Monkeys without Mothers'.

Regan, Tom, *The Case for Animal Rights* (Berkeley, Calif.: University of California Press, 1983).

Rowan, Andrew, Franklin M. Loew, and Joan C. Weer, *The Animal Research Controversy* (North Grafton, MA: Tufts Center for Animals and Public Policy, 1994).

Russell, W. M. S., and R. L. Burch, *The Principles of Humane Experimental Technique* (London: Methuen, 1959).

Singer, Peter, *Animal Liberation*, 2nd edn. (New York: New York Review of Books, 1990).

—— *Ethics into Action: Henry Spira and the Animal Rights Movement* (Lanham, MD: Rowman & Littlefield, 1998).

Smith, Jane A., and Kenneth M. Boyd (eds.), *Lives in the Balance: The Ethics of Using Animals in Biomedical Research* (Oxford: Oxford University Press, 1991).

Suomi, Stephen J., and Harry F. Harlow, 'Apparatus Conceptualization for Psychopathological Research in Monkeys', *Behavioral Research Methods and Instruments*, 1 (1969), 247–50.

—— and Harry Harlow, 'Depressive Behavior in Young Monkeys Subjected to Vertical Chamber Confinement', *Journal of Comparative and Physiological Psychology*, 180 (1972), 11–18.

Taylor, Angus, *Magpies, Monkeys, and Morals: What Philosophers Say about Animal Liberation* (Peterborough, Canada: Broadview, 1999), chapter 5: 'Is it Wrong to Use Animals for Scientific Research?'.

Wade, Nicholas, 'Animal Rights: NIH Cat Sex Study Brings Grief to New York Museum', *Science*, 194 (1976), 162–7.

Index

Visit the
VERY SHORT
INTRODUCTIONS
Web site

www.oup.co.uk/vsi

➤ **Information** about all published titles

➤ News of **forthcoming books**

➤ **Extracts** from the books, including titles
not yet published

➤ **Reviews** and views

➤ **Links** to other **web sites** and main
OUP web page

➤ Information about **VSIs in translation**

➤ **Contact** the editors

➤ **Order** other **VSIs** on-line